THE WIND-BAND AND ITS INSTRUMENTS

THEIR HISTORY, CONSTRUCTION, ACOUSTICS, TECHNIQUE AND COMBINATION

BY

ARTHUR A. CLAPPÉ

LONGWOOD PRESS
PORTLAND, MAINE

Library of Congress Cataloging in Publication Data

Clappé, Arthur A
    The wind-band and its instruments.

    Reprint of the 1911 ed. published by H. Holt,
New York.
    Includes index.
    1. Wind instruments. 2. Bands (Music)
I. Title.
ML930.C5 1976   785'.06'7   76-22327
ISBN 0-89341-011-X

Published in 1976 by LONGWOOD PRESS INC.
6 Exchange Street, Portland, Maine 04111
This Longwood Press book is an unabridged
republication of the edition of 1911.
Library of Congress Catalogue Card Number: 76-22327
International Standard Book Number: 0-89341-011-x
Printed in the United States of America

To

Major J. A. Mahan

U. S. ARMY (RETIRED),

WHOSE PROFOUND KNOWLEDGE OF ALL THINGS
PERTAINING TO THE WIND-BAND AND ITS
INSTRUMENTS IS UNRIVALED,

THIS BOOK IS INSCRIBED BY
THE AUTHOR.

PREFACE

THIS book, on the Wind-band and its instruments, must necessarily have points similar with works written concerning the orchestra, for wind instruments — at least some of them — are the coloring elements of that organization.

Again, in works treating of orchestration, wind instruments come in for consideration. Regarded from much the same point of view as the painter looks upon his colors, they are there valued accordingly and discussed in their relations as primary colors, in their blending possibilities to produce new tints, in their diffusive capacities, in their powers for vivid contrasts and for their qualities to enrich orchestra *ensemble*.

In neither instance are they dealt with as individualities of special and distinct value, but rather as parts of a whole and subordinate to string instruments. This condition results, of course, from environment. They are essentials, but aliens, and, though they may have the loudest voices, speak only by permission. Their loquacious neighbors have most to say, in fact, talk all the time and, naturally, insist upon priority of rank in their own domain.

Wind instruments have a republic of their own in the wind-band, where each one is sovereign, not subject, and all may express themselves freely, for there they are the paramount power. In this book it is sought that each instrument shall be accorded respect as befits its specific importance. For that reason, the qualities of each are taken into consideration from the viewpoints of history, acoustics, construction, technique and collective utility.

That the treatment is adequate to the importance of the subject is not claimed. On the contrary, the author believes it possible to develop the themes and make a work of larger proportions. At present, however, there is no book in the English language dealing with wind instruments and the wind-band in plan or scope herein attempted. Errors and shortcomings may exist, as inevitable with all pioneer work; but this much may be insisted, such incidents do not result from any want of desire, on the author's part, to serve the true interests of the wind-band and those who play its instruments.

CONTENTS

ILLUSTRATIONS

ILLUSTRATIONS

MUSIC IN THE TEXT

CHARTS OF FINGERING, TABLES AND DIAGRAMS

xiii

THE WIND-BAND AND ITS INSTRUMENTS

CHAPTER I

WIND AND STRING INSTRUMENTS IN GENERAL

WIND and string instruments have in all times been indispensable to certain phases of musical expression. They enter more largely into musical life to-day than at any period in the history of the art. This has been brought about by invention and development — invention of new forms and development in the facilities of older ones. Of the former may be cited the saxophone and sarrusophone; of the latter, the application of pistons to brass instruments, and, to wood wind instruments, the Boehm harmonic system. Those, together with the extension of the clarionet, by bass and contrabass; of the oboe, or bassoon family, by the contrafaggotto, and development of brass instruments in the lower bass section, are amongst the most important improvements effected. In many instances, in fact nearly all, development has preceded requirement by composers, while in a few cases new forms or extension of old ones have originated as the direct result of demand by some one of the great masters.

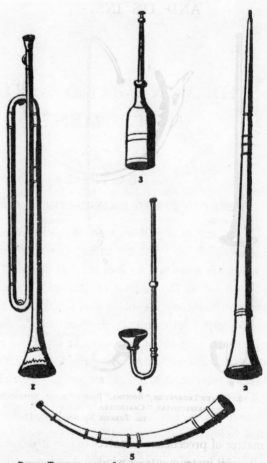

1. ROMAN TRUMPET, AFTER LUCINIUS. 2, 3, 4. CHINESE TRUMPETS.
5. ANGLO-SAXON TRUMPET.

Nevertheless, development of wind instruments, increase of expression and broadening in the realm of art are so nearly correlated as to make the difference in

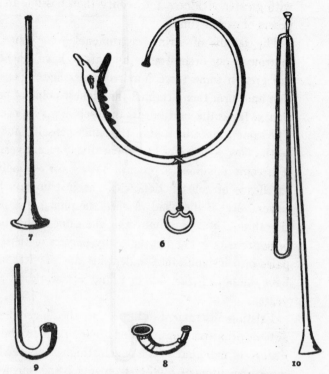

6. CURVED TRUMPET OR " BUCCINA," ROMAN. 7, 8, 9. HEBREW TRUMPETS,
RESPECTIVELY, " CHATZOZERA," " SHOPHAR," " KEREN."
10. TURKISH TRUMPET.

matter of precedence a matter of minor import, if any at
all.   All instruments — wind and string — are just as so
many colors for use by the composer.   Invention of new
and improvement of old forms have enriched his color
box and brought many new tints and shades to his palette,
thus widening his facilities for expression and extending
his powers to present ideas in more glowing contrast and

with greater vividness and reality than possible to composers of earlier times.

The family of string instruments — the bone and marrow of our orchestras — appears to have reached its full growth some three hundred years ago. Construction and form then attained the highest point of perfection, so far as the instruments themselves were concerned. The same cannot be said of their indispensable auxiliary — the bow — for only in comparatively recent years has it become possible to procure a bow corresponding in excellence of construction with the instruments themselves. But if they had reached the pinnacle of perfection three centuries or more ago, the same cannot be said of performers. The light shed by players of those days pales into insignificance under the rays of virtuosi who have illumined the fidicinal and art world in recent years.

Existing instrumental forms are the lineal descendants of primitive ones, having their origin in the early history of mankind. The conch, thigh bone, reed, etc., were progenitors of wind instruments, being transformed, in course of time, into trumpets, sackbuts (forbears of the present trombone), flutes, oboes, etc., as well as the majestic organ. From the shell of a tortoise man conceived the idea of the lyre, ravanastron, lute, crwth, viol, and so on, to our wonderfully perfect violin family. Tomtoms and other contrivances for rhythmic and signal purposes of primitive man were the ancestral stock of the family of percussion instruments of to-day. Thus, it will be seen, all instruments used in our bands and orchestras, as well as the piano and organ, were developed from the most simple elements, along the line of experiment by makers, in the first instance without aid derived from knowledge of the science of acoustics, which, later on, was applied to formulate and explain laws that, unwittingly, had been employed in their construction. In practice, the laws governing production of harmonics seem to have been recognized by players long subsequent to their enunciation by ancient philosophers who had little idea of the great use to which they would be put in our days, by composers, performers — specifically on string instruments — and makers. The wonderful possibilities of the piano and grand organ, and great facilities afforded by the Boehm system to flutes, oboes, clarionets, etc., are among the direct results of serious study and application to wind-instrument making of the science of acoustics — a science that, only in recent years, has reached its highest stage of development at the hands of Wheatstone, Helmholtz, Huxley and others.

The structure of wind instruments in the early middle ages was so very crude, it can be no cause of surprise that they were ill fitted for association, one with the other, for production of harmonious effects. Even in the days of Shakespeare, "Noise" was the English designation for a band of musicians. That the term was apt will become apparent from the statement that the common field trumpet, bugle and military fife of to-day are immeasurably superior acoustically to the wind instruments of three

hundred and fifty years back. As late as 1496 it was
"thought the neatest method of hollowing out a stick,"
required for musical purposes, was to burn through it
"with a spit."   Commenting on that fact Sir John Haw-
kins remarked, "it is not unlikely but that four hundred
years before that, an organ pipe was perforated in no
better manner; . . . we may fairly conclude that both
the organ and the music of the eleventh century were
equally rude and artificial." This side light on the
method of boring tubes very clearly shows that early
pipes, flutes, and all other instruments of the oboe kind,
were not constructed with any idea of beautiful tone
color or accurate intonation, and certainly poorly adapted
to indoor performance or combination with the more
musically voiced crwth, rebec, etc. Wind instruments
were associated with the outdoor life of the people as
accompaniment to song, or to play simple dance tunes
such as were then in vogue.

   Bands of musicians were attached to the courts of
kings and nobles as early as the reign of Edward I of
England. The following is the instrumentation of the
band of Edward III.

Trompetters 5
Cytelers 1
Pypers 5
Tabrete 1
Mabrers 1
Clarions 2
Fedeler 1
Wayghtes 3

The terms "trompette" and "pyper" need no explanation. The "citole" was a kind of dulcimer; "tabrete," a drum; "clarion," a high-voiced trumpet or bugle; "fedele," a viol or primitive fiddle, and "wayghte," an oboe. Henry, fifth Earl of Northumberland, maintained a smaller establishment, consisting of tabrete, lute and rebec, also, of course, his "trompettes." Edward IV had a band of thirteen "mynstrells," comprising "trompets, shalms and small pypes." One of the number was the "virger," "which directeth them all festyvall dayes in their statyones of blowing and pypings to such offices as the officeres might be warned to prepare for the king's meats and soupers; to be more redyere in all services and due time." As part of the allowance made to King Edward's musicians there were divided "nightelye amongeste them all iiij galanes ale." Provision was also made for servants to carry their instruments.

Bands of flute players, including soprano, alto, tenor and bass flutes, and sometimes drums, were not uncommon from the eleventh century in certain European countries. Bagpipes, and other double reed instruments, were often played in groups of greater or lesser proportions; but, generally speaking, instrumental performance was individual rather than collective before the seventeenth century. Town bands, after a fashion, were maintained in some continental towns and cities. They consisted of few performers on the zinke, cornet (a coarse-sounding reed instrument) and sackbut, combined at times with other instruments previously mentioned. Their music was traditional, played by ear, and, more often than not, in unison. These town bands had their origin in an "act of special grace" granted, in 1426, by the Emperor Sigismund to the town of Augsburg, by which its citizens were permitted to maintain a body of "town trumpeters and kettle drummers."

The nearest likeness to a modern band is to be found in the instrumentation of the one attached to the court of Bluff King Hal, otherwise King Henry VIII. For royal banquets and state functions it consisted of fourteen trumpets, ten trombones, two viols, three rebecs, one bagpipe, four tambourines and four drums. Trumpets in those days were considered the prerogative of kings and nobles, and none other might use them. They were employed for signaling, for performance of fanfares and flourishes, and upon occasions where a loud musical noise was thought necessary to add impressiveness to state or other functions.

Military bands were formed, in the reign of Louis XIV of France, of oboes, bassoons and snare drums. Following the example of Prussia, where improvements in band formation had already been made, the British Coldstream Guards, in 1783, formed a band of eight musicians, two oboes, two clarionets, two horns and two bassoons. In 1795 French bands consisted of one flute, six clarionets, three bassoons, two horns, one trumpet, one serpent and several snare drums, effecting quite an improvement over the days of Louis XIV. The foregoing shows that the military band was in an embryotic condition as late as the close of the eighteenth century.

Though clarionets had already assumed their present form and trombones and trumpets were much improved in bore and appearance, it was not until the beginning of the nineteenth century that wind instruments in their several varieties could be combined in performance with any degree of certainty of producing satisfactory results. Instrument makers of that date improved the French horn and added a slide to the trumpet. Later came the key bugle, said to have been invented by Halliday, an Englishman. Subsequently a German, Stoelzel (1820), claimed to have invented the valve. The fact appears to be that he bought the invention from an oboist, Blümel. The earliest patents taken out for the valve in England are credited to John Shaw, the first in 1824, and second, for a "rotary" or swivel action, in 1838. Though Sax, the elder (1791–1865), had effected many improvements, it is not until we arrive at the mid-career of Antoine Sax, his son (1814–1895), that evolution from the chaotic condition of wind instruments became truly apparent. He was the first to construct all brass wind-instruments on exact and scientific principles, by which close approximation to correct intonation and sympathetic unity of tone, as well as correspondence in design — as in the saxhorn family — amongst various members of the group, was secured. He improved the bore of the tubes, establishing correct dimensions, achieving better mechanical results, and so perfected valves, rotary and piston, as to make them really useful auxiliaries. His improvements and creation of the saxophone family superseded the use of serpents, ophicleides and other such weird contrivances, and inaugurated the era of the wind-band proper.

Wieprecht, the Prussian bandmaster, was doing artistically for bands what Sax had undertaken for the mechanical and scientific improvement of wind instruments. In 1838 he gave a concert at Berlin, in which sixteen infantry bands, sixteen cavalry bands and two hundred drums, in all something like 1200 players took part. Subsequently he was intrusted with the task of reorganizing the military bands of Prussia. In 1845, Spontini reorganized the French military bands along most liberal lines, including in their ranks the most important wind instruments of the day. Austria, Spain, Russia, Italy and England fell under the spell of the spirit of improvement, with the result that by the middle of the nineteenth century, wind-bands were constituted much as they are to-day.

CHAPTER II

CLASSIFICATION OF BAND INSTRUMENTS

HAVING discussed the development of instruments and "wind-bands" in a cursory manner, a more specific consideration of those employed in the latter now follows:

Band instruments are grouped in three classes, viz.: (1) Wood. (2) Brass. (3) Percussion.

"Wood" includes flute and piccolo; single-reed instruments, as clarionets and saxophones in their several dimensions; double-reed instruments, as the oboe, cor anglais, bassoon, contrabassoon and families of sarrusophones and saxophones. The two latter, excepting their mouthpieces, are made wholly of brass.

"Brass" comprises cornet, flügelhorn, trumpet, French horn, alto, baritone, or trombones (valve or slide), euphonium or B♭ bass, tuba (that is E♭ bass) and bombardon or BB♭ bass.

"Percussion" includes snare or side drum, bass drum, cymbals, triangles, glockenspiel, tambourine, castagnets and all those nondescript creations, known as "traps," used in production of descriptive music.

The foregoing classification is the one most generally accepted, but logically is incorrect, having no reason other than the constructive material to justify its use, which, as will have been noted, in case of saxophone and sarrusophone, is not accurate. A better classification would be one indicative of the influence controlling the vibrations of the air column, by which wind instruments would be divided into four classes: thus:

1. MOUTH INSTRUMENTS, as flutes and piccolo, with cylindrical tube, where the vibrations are caused by the air from the lips being broken up against the sharp edge of the mouth hole, technically *embouchure*.

2. INSTRUMENTS PLAYED WITH A SINGLE REED, in which the column of air is set in vibration by means of a single reed attached to the mouthpiece by a ligature. This group includes clarionets and saxophones, which are as important in the band as are string instruments in the orchestra. The clarionet tube is cylindrical, while that of the saxophone is conical. Thus the clarionet acts somewhat as a stopped pipe and the saxophone as an open one, in relation to their harmonics or overtones.

3. INSTRUMENTS PLAYED WITH A DOUBLE REED, wherein the air column is set in motion by vibration of that adjunct, as the oboe, cor anglais, bassoon and sarrusophones, the first three made of wood, the last of brass. These instruments have conical tubes in common, the smaller end being that where the reed is affixed. The harmonics of this group are those usual in all open tubes.

4. INSTRUMENTS PLAYED WITH A CUPPED MOUTHPIECE. In this group the player's lips act as reeds and thereby impart a vibratory motion to the air column. Pressure of the mouthpiece against the lips, conjointly with normal, increased or relaxed tension, determine speed of vibration

and account for height or depth of resulting sounds. This group includes trumpet, horn, cornet, flügelhorn, trombone, alto, baritone or euphonium, E♭ tuba, B♭ and BB♭ basses, the six last mentioned belonging to the saxhorn family. The harmonics or overtones follow in similar order from the fundamental sound of each, though not in extent, in all the foregoing. The tube is conical on all the above, excepting the trumpet and trombone, where it is cylindrical to the bell joint. All cupped-mouthpiece instruments, irrespective of shape of tube, have a conical enlargement, otherwise "bell," the three last mentioned having it in one-third their length. The proportions of the bell are said to affect the accuracy of the harmonics.

The shape of the mouthpiece, together with dimensions of tube, are potent in determining the quality of tone in the several instruments of this class. Roughly stated a "cup," approximating a hemisphere in shape, is more or less blatant, as the throat or orifice (the narrowest part of the mouthpiece), through which the breath passes into the instrument, is near or further removed from the lips. The more nearly the cup approaches the cone shape, the sweeter will be the tone produced. A somewhat elongated cone, as in the case of the horn mouthpiece, assists and in fact is essential to formation of a soft, velvety voice. As instruments vary in length and internal dimensions of tubing, so do mouthpieces differ in size, the cup being, of course, larger for deep-sounding instruments than for those emitting tones in higher scales. It will be perceived that the inner shape of the mouthpiece exercises a great influence on tone character, a fact pointing to the moral, that selection of a mouthpiece must not be made haphazard or whimsically, but, on the contrary, governed by the law of eternal fitness.

Finally, dimension, that is, diameter of tubing, affects tone character, as is apparent in the difference of tone subsisting between trumpet, trombone and horn, with long narrow tubes, and the saxhorn family of corresponding pitch, whose tubes are of wider diameter. The reason of this is greater richness of harmonics of the narrow tube, as against their paucity in those of more ample dimension, resulting in greater clarity and purity of tone in the former than in the latter.

5. INSTRUMENTS OF PERCUSSION. This group has already been referred to. It is only necessary to add that this class may be divided into those with *definable resonance*, as kettledrums, bells, etc., and those with *indefinable resonance*, as the side or snare drum, bass drum, cymbal, etc.

The foregoing grouping shows five classes of instruments in use in the band, which, again, may be arranged in family groups according to their distinguishing tone color.

1. Flutes and piccolos in all degrees of pitch.
2. Clarionets, including those in A, B, C, E♭, etc., alto clarionet in F, bass clarionet and contrabass clarionet.
3. Saxophones, including soprano, alto, tenor and baritone.
4. Oboe, cor anglais, oboe d'amour (rarely used), bassoon and contrabassoon.
5. Sarrusophones, soprano, alto, tenor, baritone and contrabass; invented (*Circa* 1856) by the French bandmaster, Sarrus.

6. Trumpets, trombones of all kinds, tenor and bass, slide or valve.

7. The cornet, uniting in some degree the characteristics of class 6 with those of class 8.

8. Saxhorns. This family comprises seven members, viz.: (1) E♭ sopranino, (2) B♭ soprano, (3) E♭ alto, (4) B♭ baritone, (5) B♭ bass, (6) E♭ tuba, (7) BB♭ bass. The alto, baritone, B♭ bass, E♭ tuba and BB♭ bass are all used in American bands. The B♭ soprano should be, it being superior in tone quality to the cornet, with which it is identical in pitch.

9. Flügelhorn is the modern form of the old key bugle. Its pitch is similar with the cornet and soprano saxhorn. By reason of the wider diameter of its tubes, its tone color is less like the former than the latter, with which it is, on that account, nearer of kin.

All the foregoing cupped-mouthpiece instruments are equipped with pistons, used to fill the spaces between notes of the series of natural harmonics. They were invented by Blümel, a Silesian (1815), and applied first to the horn; but Sax, a Belgian maker residing at Paris about 1845, improved them into their present form. The slide trombone is the only exception to the foregoing; its slide, pushed outward or drawn inward at will, fulfills the same purpose as do the pistons. The slide trumpet has become obsolete.

10. Percussion instruments of definable resonance, pair of kettledrums or tympani, each being tuned, note by note, to create usually the interval of a fourth or fifth between the two, as circumstances may require; glockenspiel, xylophone, tubular pipes, metal bars to imitate small and large bells, all of fixed pitch. Each of the four last named has a complete chromatic scale.

11. Percussion instruments of indefinable resonance, as the snare or side drum, bass drum, tomtom, cymbals, triangle, gong, tambourine, castagnets, etc. Under the general title of traps are included cocoanut shells to imitate the beats of a horse's hoofs, sand paper and sheet-iron contrivances to imitate wind, rain, thunder, etc., as well as those more musical affairs to imitate birds and so on.

In conclusion, it may be stated that the material from which wind instruments are made has no influence on their tone quality, their sonority existing in the air column within their tubes.   Brass instruments are made of that metal for reason of its ductility, which lends itself readily to any form of structure.   Repeated experiments have shown that instruments made of gutta percha, plaster of paris, wood or any other material, have quite as good tone as those devised from brass, providing hardness, density, diameter, length and finish be equal in each.

CHAPTER III

ON THE ACOUSTICS OF WIND INSTRUMENTS

MUSICAL sounds may be defined as "the effect produced on the brain by transmission through the ear and the auditory nerves, by the successive striking of waves of air on the drum of the ear."

"When a column of air contained in an open tube is set in vibration by the lips, it produces a series of waves, the length of which can never be greater than the length of the tube which holds the air. If the air in the tube vibrate as a whole, from end to end, the sound produced is called the fundamental sound. If the pressure of the lips be increased, the column of air can be made to vibrate in two, three, four, five or more equal parts, and the waves thus produced in the air will be in length $\frac{1}{2}$, $\frac{1}{3}$, $\frac{1}{4}$, $\frac{1}{5}$, etc., of the open tube. The sounds produced by causing the column of air in the tube to vibrate in these different parts are called the harmonics of the fundamental sound." — *Mahan.*

Thus, whatever the nominal pitch of an open pipe, if it be sounded in its entire length, the fundamental, or lowest tone of its scale will result. In practical band work, on the smaller instruments, emission of those fundamental tones is impossible. The lowest sound of the tube usually produced on instruments with cupped mouthpieces is the

17

first harmonic of the fundamental tone, otherwise its octave, excepting on those with wide diameter, as the B♭ bass, on which the fundamental is more easily obtained. Cornet soloists, however, often bring out the fundamental tone for purposes of effect.

Instruments with cupped mouthpieces are the simplest form of consonant tubes, varying in length from 3 feet 7½ inches to 19 feet 4¼ inches. The French horn (C low) has a length of about 17 feet. The method of exciting the vibration of the air column within their tubes is the same in all instruments of this class. "At the smaller extremity is the cup, forming an expansion of the bore, carrying a rounded edge against which the tense lips of the player are steadily pressed. The reed thus constituted is of the membranous kind, not dissimilar to the vocal cords of the human larynx. The method of its vibration is totally different from the reed of the oboe or clarionet; for, whereas in these the lower harmonic notes are damped by the appended tube and one of the higher and sweeter partials reinforced, in the cupped instruments every successive harmonic from the very lowest is practicable, and all but the extreme bass sounds are actually used successively in producing the scale. The sequence of sounds in the harmonic series, modified slightly according to the particular instrument, depends for its production entirely on the varied tension of the lips, and is commonly termed the scale of Open Notes. It is to bridge over the long gaps and intervals between these open notes that all systems of valves, slides and keys are intended. The natural or open notes are as follows in the French horn, which furnishes the most perfect example of the class.

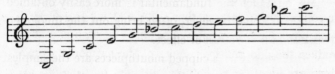

"It will be seen that in the lower part of the series the intervals between the sounds are large, but that the upper harmonics approach closer and closer together, so that from the middle B♭ a nearly perfect octave scale of continuous notes can be obtained." — *Stone*.

It should be observed that the notes B♭ are not in tune with those of our artificial scale of equal temperament. Those sounds, and others where variation appeared, were corrected; and the missing notes required to complete the scale, diatonic and chromatic, were obtained in former days by thrusting the hand into the bell of the French horn, "and so lowering the pitch by a variable quantity." The adaptation of valves has now very largely superseded that employment of the hand. In the case of the trumpet, which, speaking an octave higher, produces the first eleven open notes of the series given above, and the trombone, slides were, and in the latter case still are, used, thereby enabling the player to obtain all chromatic semitones at will.

In connection with the subject of the vibration of air columns it is desirable to note that they vibrate in segments corresponding with those of a vibrating string.

Increased pressure has the same effect upon the air waves as that of dividing and subdividing the string, excepting that the direction of the oscillations differ; those of the air column being lateral, those of the string transverse. Open pipes have invariably a segment at each end and produce the odd and even tones of the harmonic series, which are identical with those obtained by divisions of the string.

The flute, oboe, bassoon, and other instruments of their class, the saxophone and sarrusophone, are all open pipes, uttering the harmonic series in sequence similar with, but differing in pitch, from that already given. Thus, "a skillful flute player, making no alteration in the fingering of the holes, but altering the character of his blast, can produce not only the first note but any one of several of its harmonics." — *Airy*.

All soprano cupped-mouthpiece instruments (excepting the French horn) nominally give ⟨staff⟩ as their first open sound, the same being ⟨staff⟩ an octave higher than the fundamental. Consequently the series of "open" sounds or harmonics expressed in writing for one covers all; thus —

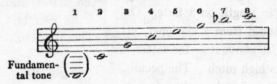

But as instruments in A, B♭, E♭, F, etc., are used, it must be remembered that the C above given is nominal only, not actual, the true sound being that from which the instrument is named.

Inasmuch as the first open sound of all bass instruments, for instance B♭, G or F trombones, B♭ and E♭ basses, corresponds with the actual pitch, it is a matter simply of transposition to obtain a plan of the open sound, or harmonic series suitable to each in accordance with its pitch name.

The seventh note of the series above given is not in tune with the B♭ of our scale of equal temperament and therefore not available in practice.

The clarionet differs from other instruments in the nature of its harmonics, having the characteristics of a stopped pipe.

"The stopped pipe of an organ is merely a pipe with a plug at the end, or cap upon it, so that the wind has to travel to and fro to obtain an exit at the open lip, or notch. The column of air is thus doubled in length and the note produced is therefore an octave lower than that of an open pipe. A clarionet is of the nature of a stopped pipe, and although closed only at the end next the mouth, the effect of lowering the tone by an octave is the same. One foot in length of the clarionet produces the same C as two feet in length on a flute. Only two harmonics can be produced from a clarionet, viz.: a twelfth and another twelfth above it — the latter, with difficulty, on account of its high pitch. The peculiar harmonics of the clarionet were first brought into notice by Sir Charles Wheatstone, F. R. S." — *Chappell.*

The sounds above referred to are

Professor Tyndall, following Helmholtz, says, " The clarionet has the harmonics 1, 3, 5, 7, by opening the holes at the side." This statement is based on the principle that stopped pipes in general produce the odd-number harmonics of the open-pipe. series. "Opening the holes at the side" of a clarionet is, as Chappell remarks, "to change the fundamental note " and introduce a principle in disagreement with that applied to the open tube. From this it will be noticed, the clarionet stands in a class peculiar to itself.

It was an old theory that no difference of pitch could subsist between pipes of equal length unless one of them chanced to be a stopped pipe, as width was supposed only to increase loudness. Modern practice proves the existence of such a variation. When pipes are but two to three feet long the variation is very small, but in larger pipes increase of diameter appreciably flattens the pitch. For instance, by reason of its great diameter — 15 inches — a pipe 28 feet 6 inches in length is found in practice to produce a 32-foot tone, having 16 vibrations to the second. A similar effect shows itself in wind-instrument making. For, "if it is desired to enlarge a tenor horn so as to acquire a baritone quality of tone, the tube of the former being 6 feet 6 inches in length will only be shortened by one inch, although the diameter is increased by several sizes. And yet, on the other hand, there will be a variation of one inch and a half in the length of two horns of small size, to produce the same note from both. The actual scale for horns having two-thirds of cylindrical tube and the lowest third of conical form ending in a bell is as follows:

Tube $\frac{1}{2}$-inch diameter, length $40\frac{1}{4}$ inches, sounds A$\natural$.

Tube $\frac{7}{16}$-inch diameter, length $41\frac{3}{4}$ inches, sounds A$\natural$.

Difference of form of the two cones may be one cause of the variation, for the more dilated the cone, the flatter the pitch. But there are so many bearings in these cases that the subject is one of considerable difficulty." — *Chappell.*

Drums are described as instruments "in which a stretched disk of elastic parchment is struck with a stick. In the big drum and side drum no musical note is aimed at; but in the kettledrum used in the orchestra the parchment can, by screws on the circumference, be given different degrees of tension, which, on the principle explained for strings, will give different degrees of pitch. In this drum also the membrane is stretched over a hollow cavity which acts as a resounding chamber and considerably improves the tone."

Most of the instruments depending on the percussion of solid bodies for their vibration, such as tuning forks, triangles, cymbals, xylophones, elastic metal bars or bells so called, "give rise to what may be called irregular overtones, having inharmonic relations to the fundamental.

For example, the first overtone of a tuning fork gives an undefined variable note, vibrating somewhere between 5.8 and 6.6 times as fast as the fundamental, and the others are equally inharmonic."

"The subsidiary tones thus produced are called *inharmonic* overtones; and the compound sounds which contain them lose in proportion as they prevail, the satisfactory character of musical tones normally constituted: for which reason their use in music can only be tolerated when the fundamental largely predominates, and even then only with certain precautions." — *Pole*.

The foregoing offers some explanation why the attempt to play the metal-bar bells — or any other — employed in band or orchestra, in harmony of third, sixth and so on, is never satisfactory to the critical ear.

CHAPTER IV

DISCREPANCIES OF TUNE IN PISTON INSTRUMENTS

BEFORE proceeding to the consideration of instruments individually, historically, technically and elsewise, it is necessary to point out some of the defects incidental to the application and use of pistons. These defects are inseparable from, and emphasize the limitations imposed by, the piston system of structure, especially when employed in combinations, as they must be, to facilitate production of complete scales and the performance of music as now written for the several instruments.

The slide trombone shows the basic principle underlying the invention and application of pistons. But, while that instrument will utter tones at accurate pitch, in the descending chromatic scale from its first position, by successive lengthenings or "shifts" of its tube, the pistons of other instruments, designed to effect similar lengthenings, do so only approximately when combinations of those pistons become necessary, as they frequently do. In rapid passages discrepancies of intonation are passed unnoticed, but in slow movements and sustained harmonies they become distinctly apparent, unless the performer, by use of ear and lips, corrects them. In this instance, as in many others, to be forewarned is to be

29

forearmed, for which reason players on piston instruments should be acquainted from the outset with those discrepancies and the cause of their existence.

Each piston controls a certain length of tubing, attached to the instrument and through which the air may be caused to pass, when the air-way is opened by pressing the piston down. The second piston controls tubing sufficient to add a half tone to the length of the normal tube; the first piston a full tone, and third piston a tone and one-half. By combinations of two with three, one with three, and one and two with three, still further lengthenings can be effected, thus descending to the lowest tone practicable on the instrument, which in every instance, on three-valve instruments, is a sound at the interval of an augmented fourth, or diminished fifth, as it may be variously expressed, from the first open sound of the instrument, thus:

To bass instruments, such as the B♭ bass, E♭ bass and even BB♭ bass, a fourth piston has been added.

"It is a well-known principle of acoustics that the number of vibrations per second furnished by the fundamental sound or by any harmonic of an air column is, for the same diameter, inversely proportional to the length of the column. That is to say, the longer the column the fewer the number of vibrations per second. This relation between vibrations and length makes the discussion of the question a simple one, because dimensions, which are visible, can be used instead of vibrations, which are invisible. Let it be stated here that all dimensions and numbers of vibrations used here are given on the basis of the international standard pitch; that is, the having 870 single, or 435 double vibrations per second. On this basis the length of the open tube of the B♭ cornet is 4 feet 9.98 inches. The length required for A is 5 feet 1.54 inches. The difference between these two lengths is 3.56 inches, which is the length required for the second additional tube. The length of tube required for A♭ is 5 feet 5.20 inches. Subtracting from this the length of the B♭ tube there is obtained 7.22 inches as the length of the first additional tube, which corresponds to the whole tone B♭–A♭. The length of the air column required for the G tube is 5 feet 9.06 inches. Subtracting from this the length of the B♭ air column, the remainder is 11.08 inches, which is the length of the third additional tube. Now, if the lengths of the second and first additional tubes be added together, the sum is 10.78 inches, which is three-tenths of an inch less than the length of the third tube, hence the sound obtained from the two tubes is sharp, as compared with that obtained from the third tube, by almost exactly one-twelfth of a semitone. So, if two cornets were to hold for some time a sustained note, one of them with the third piston and the other with the first and second pistons, the difference would be perceived after a certain time, but for the ordinary needs of playing the two ways of taking the same note would pass unnoticed except by a keener ear than that of the great majority of bandsmen and bandmasters. Pistons 1 and 2 together

are a little sharp as compared with piston 3, consequently
when the rule is laid down that pistons 1 and 2 must give
the same sound as piston 3 when the instrument is in tune,
it amounts to saying that either 1 or 2, or both of them,
must be flat, or that piston 3 must be sharp. Such a
rule is absurd for any three-piston instrument made in
the ordinary way; and the absurdity arises from the
very nature of the instrument itself. To obtain the
F♯, written [♪], pistons 2 and 3 must be used. The
true length [♪] of tube required for this F♯ is 6 feet
1.19 inches. The length obtained by the pistons is:

Length of the natural tube....................	4 ft.	9.98 in.
" " 2nd additional tube...............	....	3.56 "
" " 3rd " "	....	11.08 "
Total	6 ft.	0.62 in.

which is 0.57 inch too short, almost one-sixth of the length
of the second additional tube, and hence nearly a twelfth
of a tone high. This borders very closely on the line of
intolerance. Still it, too, may be allowed to pass. For
F♮, written [♪], pistons 1 and 3 are needed. The
true length [♪] of tube required for this F is 6 feet
5.51 inches. The length obtained by the piston is:

Length of natural tube......................	4 ft.	9.98 in.
" " 1st additional tube................	....	7.22 "
" " 3rd " "	....	11.08 "
Total..............................	6 ft.	4.28 in.

which is 1.23 inch too short, slightly more than one-third
of the length of the second additional tube, or more than
one-seventh of a tone sharp. So this combination is

inadmissible except in rapid successions of notes, where the ear has not time to take in the falsity of the sound. For E, written ♪, all three pistons must be used. The true length ♪ of tube required for this E is 6 feet 10.17 inches. The length obtained by the pistons is:

Length of natural tube......................	4 ft.	9.98 in.
" " 2nd additional tube...............	....	3.56 "
" " 1st " "	....	7.22 "
" " 3rd " "	....	11.08 "
Total.........................	6 ft.	7.84 in.

which is 2.33 inches too short, very nearly two-thirds of the length of the second additional tube, or, rather, more than quarter of a tone sharp. This is inadmissible except in a very rapid passage, where this combination would be scarcely more than touched. Fortunately, of the thirty-one notes which form the ordinary scale of the instruments with three pistons, from ♪ to ♪ as written, only eight require the use of more than one piston, and of these eight four are made with pistons 2 and 3, which, as has been seen, will pass; while only two, ♪ and ♪, are made with 1 and 3; and two, ♪ and ♪, are made with all three pistons. These four notes should be avoided if possible. In very rapid successions of notes, like scales and trills, they are permissible, thanks to the imperfections of the ear. The question which naturally presents itself

is this: Can these defects be rectified? The answer is,
They can be greatly diminished, but they cannot be
wholly removed. To explain this the more intelligently
let the written notes be substituted for the true sounds,
bearing in mind that the latter are a tone lower than the
written notes. The lowest sound of the open tube of
the cornet is that represented by [musical notation]. The second
piston gives [musical notation], the first [musical notation] piston, [musical notation],
the third [musical notation] piston, [musical notation]. It has
been shown that the com- [musical notation] bination of pistons
1 and 2 is in error by about one-twelfth of a semitone,
a defect so slight that it can be neglected. This being
so, it is superfluous to have two ways of making the same
note, especially as the third piston gives such poor results
in two of the three combinations which it can make with
the other pistons. Suppose now that the third additional
tube be tuned to give a major third instead of a minor
third below the open tube, the notation for the third
piston will be [musical notation] instead of [musical notation]. This gives
the length of [musical notation] the third [musical notation] additional
tube, in this case 15.21 inches. To obtain the written
[musical notation] pistons 3 and 2 would have to be used. This
[musical notation] combination gives:

Length of natural tube......................	4 ft.	9.98 in.
" " 3rd additional tube...............	1 "	3.21 "
" " 2nd " "	....	3.56 "
Total............................	6 ft.	4.75 in.

But the length of tube required for this G (true sound F♮)
is 6 feet 5.51 inches, hence the combination is only 0.76

inch too short, or a little less than one-eleventh of a tone
sharp. This is a great improvement over the G (true
sound F♮) obtained before. That was more than one-
seventh of a tone sharp, this one is *less* than one-eleventh; this can be admitted as sufficiently satisfactory
and a good and are obtained. For
the written or the first and third additional tubes are needed, and the length so obtained is:

	ft.	in.
Length of natural tube	4 ft.	9.98 in.
" " 3rd additional tube	1 "	3.21 "
" " 1st " "	....	7.22 "
Total	6 ft.	8.41 in.

But the length of tube required for the true sound (E) is
6 feet 10.17 inches, hence the combination of tubes is too
short by 1.76 inch. This is a little less than one-fifth of
a tone high, a little better than what was had with the
other combination of pistons, more than quarter of a tone,
but still unsatisfactory. To add the second additional
tube would give a sound very much too flat. The only
method of having a good and consequently a good
(both written), is to add a fourth piston
tuned to the F♯, or a diminished fifth below the
natural tube. If this piston were added to the cornet,
or to any other instrument of similar construction, there
need be no interference with the ordinary fingering of the
instrument for general use, but in cantabile playing or in
sustained notes the two notes given above would be true.

Having then an instrument with four pistons tuned as
follows: 1st piston, a major tone; 2nd piston, a semitone; 3rd piston, a major third; 4th piston, a diminished
fifth below the open tube, there would be had a complete
scale, satisfactory to the ear from the lowest to the highest note.   There is one danger to be feared in the addition
of the fourth additional tube and piston, viz., that composers and arrangers, not understanding or not troubling
themselves to study the true use of this addition, would
misuse it, as they have done with the fourth piston of
the B♭ bass, to continue a so-called scale downward from
♩ to ♩ , in which all the intermediate notes
are false, without exception, the inaccuracy increasing with each semitone, until it reaches
very nearly a half tone at the ♩ , which is nearly
a whole tone higher than ♩ the ♩ , which
is the fundamental of the instrument, and which
is true.   The real use of the fourth piston is to give
an accurately tuned F♯, and not to extend downward
the compass of any instrument.   When it is necessary
to descend below this, an instrument of lower pitch
should be used.   It is not likely that an instrument with
four pistons tuned as above indicated will soon be made.
Prejudice on the part of performers will alone suffice to
make such a change next to impossible.   The falsity of
intonation due to the combination of pistons can be
corrected, within limits only, by the lips of the performer.
To secure this result much time and practice are required.
No mechanical means can correct a defect inherent in the

very nature of the instrument. Two and two can never make four-and-a-half, no matter how much time and ingenuity may be expended in trying to produce a mechanism to accomplish this result. So the combination of two or more pistons will never, under the general form of construction, produce any other than a tone which is more or less sharp. The piston instruments are like all other instruments, there is none which is perfect. The player's individuality must enter into his work, and individuality requires more study and greater care in its development than does anything else. When Rossini was asked what were the three most necessary qualities for a singer, he replied: 'The first is voice; the second is voice; the third is voice.' With the player it may be said that the first necessity is work; the second is work; the third is work. Work continuous and incessant is the price which one must pay for success; and, other things being equal, the player who works the hardest to overcome the natural defects of his instrument — to overcome, for they can never be eradicated — is the one to whom will come honor and distinction." — *Mahan.*

In conclusion, it may be remarked, the fourth piston as employed by all modern makers, increases the length of the normal tube sufficient to obtain a perfect fourth below the first open sound usually recognized, although by reason of the wide dimension of tubing the fundamental sound is more easily obtainable on instruments such as the B♭ bass than on those of narrower bore, as has already been pointed out. The combinations of that piston, possible with others, affords additional facilities in "fingering," and enables the player to produce chromatic semitones in the lower range, impossible on a three-valve instrument. Those notes, as Major Mahan has pointed out in a preceding paragraph, are much out of tune. The greatest care must, therefore, be used in their production. To correct them, some makers have added a fifth piston, by use of which the notes of the gap between the fundamental tone and its octave may be played with greater approximation to correct pitch. The fifth piston simplifies the fingering in some instances and renders trills possible, which, heretofore, had been impossible.

CHAPTER V

ON FORMATION OF WIND-BANDS

THE orchestra, through length of years of service and writings of great composers, has acquired a settled or conventional form. The band, younger in the art world, never taken seriously by the masters, is still chaotic, no agreement having yet been reached as to numbers, combinations of individual or families of instruments requisite to create an organization, that shall, to their limitations, fulfill the demands of art and become satisfying to composers and connoisseurs. Every bandmaster appears to be a law unto himself in the matter of tonal balance and proprieties (or improprieties) of band formation. Few, if any, recognize that homogeneity can only be accomplished by philosophical consideration of the mechanical, acoustical nature of wind instruments, as well as the æsthetic quality of their tones, and the adaptation of the principles gained from such consideration to the elements of the organizations under their control. The nearest approach to established order is to be found among government or military bands, so called. But even there, if we take a survey of the usage in different countries, we shall find wide divergencies. Regulation by law of the number of players and instrumentation is the prerogative of governments, but that the same is ap-

propriate or logical, viewed by art standards, is a wide-
open question. Bands formed for military service should
be distinguished by virile sonority. For that reason it
might be supposed that brass-wind and percussion instruments exclusively would be employed. Yet what do we
find? In American government bands, regulated at
twenty-four members, are employed about three-fourths
brass, never organized with consideration for family grouping, and one-fourth reed, including piccolo; which gives
just sufficient reed color to disturb and of course not
enough to be of artistic value. Further, from the point
of view of virility, the army band loses about one-sixth of
its tone power by the incorporation of the "reed" element. The employment of reed instruments in our army
bands is a concession to military social requirement. It
being admitted that such is necessary — and there can
be no doubt on that point — the better way to meet it
would be to increase the strength of our army bands to
forty players, which number would allow for a properly
balanced reed section and make the band tonally strong
enough to meet all demands on the march.

On the other hand there exist concert bands, so called,
in which the assortment of instruments appear to have
been drawn together for variety and without consideration of appropriateness. Bands of more or less reputa-
tion, awarded by an uncritical public, are not uncommon
in which we find incomplete families of reed instruments,
for instance clarionets without their alto, bass and contrabass kin, and E♭ alto saxophones, lacking their comple-

ment of soprano, baritone and bass. Again, trumpets are rarely found, and certain valuable members of the saxhorn family, as well as the flügelhorn, are actually tabooed.

The military bands, so called, of our towns and villages, are nondescript organizations. They are more often than not the manifestation of good will toward music on the part of certain members of the community, but just as frequently they are exhibitions of the inefficacy of good will without proper direction. Cacophony is hardly the term to apply to the performance of many of them; the noise in a boiler-maker's shop is harmony by comparison. And yet the fault is hardly theirs. Rather is it attributable to lack of instruction, example and indifference of a public that has yet failed to perceive the art potentialities latent in the wind-band. If indifference of the public must be condemned, the obtuseness and lack of foresight on the part of composers of note are worthy of double condemnation; for in these days, when a high degree of perfection obtains throughout the several groups of instruments from which an excellent wind-band might be formed, more than equal in musical resources with the orchestra, their failure to write for such is obviously gross neglect, for which the only excuse that may be offered in extenuation is want of precedent.

The homogeneity of the orchestra is the result of the harmonious combination of its elements. In other words, it is a picture in which the string color predominating, the tints and shades of other instruments impart richness and variety, emphasizing by relief the stronger color without marring or detracting from its value. The concert band might be made equally homogeneous were clarionets employed, complete in their class or family, in proportion and manner, comparable with the string family in the orchestra. The string quintet is the backbone of the orchestra; the clarionet quintet should be considered as the vertebræ of the concert band. Numerically, clarionets should preponderate; first, second and third clarionets, alto clarionets and bass clarionets being employed in proportions equal with the first and second violins, violas and celli of the orchestra. The contrabass clarionet might be used to complete the choir, for special effects, or to assist in imparting a "reedy" quality to the band; but for the foundation bass, the tuba and BB♭ bass must necessarily be the constant element. E♭ clarionets would, in such an arrangement, be employed to strengthen the B♭ clarionets in sonorous passages, and to carry out motives in the upper ranges lying beyond the compass of the latter. For practical purposes they would be considered primarily as instruments of extension. Surrounding the clarionets, as it were, piccolo, flute, oboe, bassoon and all brass instruments would contribute the effect of their special tone color, enhancing their effect as the central figure of the organization.

To impart additional color, strengthen the impression of "reediness," and assist in amalgamation of clarionet tone with that of the brass, with characteristics peculiarly their own, a quartet of saxophones would appear almost indispensable. This finely voiced family of instruments is not appreciated as it should be. As a special choir, or in combinations, it is most expressive, and worthy of the serious consideration of composers and bandmasters. Of the sarrusophone group, very little used, the alto and baritone could be employed effectively to supplement the bassoons in sonorous passages. Similarly the soprano sarrusophone might be used to supplement the oboe and, finally, the contrabass sarrusophone would be found of great value in adding sonority and agility to the bass section. In this connection it is pertinent to remark that the contrabass clarionet, sarrusophone and bassoon, used conjointly with the ordinary brass basses — which might be reduced in number — would give an effect of sonority without blatancy, and more comparable with the string bass tone, than now obtains by the present, almost exclusive, usage of brass basses with cupped mouthpiece.

By reason of the greater sonority of clarionets, as against violins, oboes and bassoons should be used in double quantity in the band, or supplemented, as previously suggested, by members of the sarrusophone group, not by saxophones, as is sometimes the case. The tone of the latter does not suggest the piquancy of the double-reed oboe or the lugubriousness of the bassoon.

Following out the suggestion of kinship, cornets might still be used, but it would be preferable to employ trumpets, forming a choir with the trombones, to which they are very nearly related by reason of similarity of tube, mouthpiece and, above all, tone color. Their range of compass and flexibility of manipulation are equal with those of the cornet, to which they are much superior in virility and brilliancy of tone. Bands are to be congratulated on the increasing tendency to use B♭ trumpets instead of B♭ cornets. The "choir" formed by the trumpet family consists of B♭ and E♭ trumpets, B♭ tenor trombone and G or F bass trombone.

The French horn stands unique among brass instruments for compass and beautiful velvety quality of tone. It is employed in concert bands in quartet of first, second, third and fourth, and is inimitable in adaptability for special effects, where soft, sweet, tender, pastoral motives are to be depicted, in jocund hunting strains, or in their power of sustaining harmonies and thus cementing, by their blending quality of tone, the whole harmonic structure. They assimilate with both reed and brass better, perhaps, than any other cupped-mouthpiece instruments.

Saxhorns are seven in number, viz.: E♭ sopranino, B♭ soprano, E♭ alto, B♭ baritone, B♭ bass, E♭ bass and BB♭ bass. The baritone and B♭ bass differ only, in that the latter has tubing of greater dimension than the former, by reason of which its low notes are fuller and easier of utterance, but, on the other hand, high notes are harder to produce than on the first named. The E♭ sopranino, excepting in France and Belgium, has given way to the E♭ cornet in brass bands; the B♭ soprano saxhorn is likewise superseded by the cornet, which artistically has much less merit; otherwise, with occasionally more or less modification peculiar to different makers for business reasons, the remaining members of the saxhorn family are to be found in our bands.

The flügelhorn is a descendant of the old key bugle. It was so named (fugelhorn or flügelhorn) from the fact that the player of that instrument in German regimental brass bands marched at the right-hand corner of the front rank and was known as *flügelmann*. The instrument, in quality of tone, is broader than the cornet. Its tubing is of wider dimensions. Hence its lower notes come out more freely, for which reason it would, at least, be more effective than second and third cornets.

Of percussion instruments it is only necessary to say their number should be limited and use confined to occasional and specific effects. It would seem as though bandmasters, or other persons responsible for the formation of some of our bands, were warm admirers of the Janissary music of the Turkish army, where predominance of shrill tones and clangorous reverberations of gongs, cymbals, etc., and drums are keenly relished. The pernicious custom of attaching one cymbal to the bass drum to be struck by its fellow in the left hand of the drummer should be checked. It is ruinous alike to tone of cymbal and drum. Also the practice of employing cymbals constantly, whenever the bass drum is used, has nothing to commend it. On the contrary, it is retrogression. It links us with the savage rhythmic impulse of a primitive age.

THE WIND–BAND

The following table gives examples of the composition of bands in various countries.

Instruments.	Germany.	Austria.	France.	Russia.	England.	Italy.	United States (Sousa).
Piccolo and Flute, D♭ ..	1	1	1	1	1	1	1
Concert Flute..........		1	1	1	1	1	1
Oboes...............	2	......	2	......	2	2	2
Clarionet, E♭..........	2	1	1	1	2	1	2
Clarionet, B♭..........	8	8	8	8	10	8	12
Clarionet, Alto........	......	......	......	2	1	......	1
Clarionet, Bass........	......	......	......	......	1	......	1
Clarionet, Contrabass..	......	......	......	......	......	......	....
Saxophone, Soprano....	......	......	1	......	......	1	....
Saxophone, Alto ,.....	......	......	1	......	......	1	1
Saxophone, Tenor......	......	......	1	......	......	1	1
Saxophone, Bass.......	......	......	1	......	......	......	1
Bassoon.............	2	......	2	......	2	2	2
Bassoon, Contra-......	......	......	......	......	......	1	....
Cornets, B♭ or E♭......	2 E♭	......	2	......	4	{ 1 E♭ / 3 B♭ }	4
Flügelhorn...........	2 {	6 / 2 Bass }	2	2	....	2	....
Trumpets.............	4	12	2	4 to 8	2	4	2
French horns.........	4	4	2	4	4	4	....
Alto horns, E♭........	......	......	3	......	2	......	....
Baritone, B♭..........	2	......	2	......	1	2	2
Trombones...........	4	......	3	......	3	4	4
Euphonium or B♭ Bass.	......	......	1	2	1	2	2
Bass, E♭............. }	3	3 in F	1	2	2	1	....
Bass, BB♭........... }	......	3	1	......	2	1	2
Percussion instruments.	3	4	3	3	3	6	4

Note. — One or two contrabassoons are often added in Germany. One A♭ clarionet is used in Germany and Austria.

The above table, excepting Sousa's band, showing considerable divergency, is compiled from Kalkbrenner's " Bands in all Lands."

CLASSIFICATION OF THE WIND-BAND.

Instruments.	18	20	22	24	26	27	29	32	34	35	36	37	38	40	41	42	43	44	45	46	48	51	53	55	57	59	61	62
Piccolo	1	1	1	1	1	1	1	1	1	1	1	1	1	1	1	1	1	1	1	1	1	1	1	1	1	1	1	1
Flutes	1	1	1	1	1	1	1	1	2	2	2	2	2	2	2	2	2	2	2	2	2	2	2	2	2	2	2	2
Eb Clarionets	1	1	1	1	1	1	1	2	2	2	2	2	2	2	2	2	2	2	2	2	2	2	2	2	2	2	2	2
Oboes	1	1	1	1	1	1	1	2	2	2	2	2	2	2	2	2	2	2	2	2	2	2	2	2	6	6	6	6
1st Bb Clarionets	3	3	3	3	3	3	3	4	4	4	4	4	4	4	4	4	4	5	5	5	5	4	4	4	4	4	4	4
2d Bb Clarionets	2	2	2	2	2	2	2	2	3	3	3	3	3	3	3	3	3	3	3	3	3	3	3	3	3	3	3	3
3d Bb Clarionets	1	1	1	1	1	1	1	2	2	2	2	2	2	3	2	3	3	3	3	3	3	3	3	3	3	3	3	3
1st Cornets	2	2	2	2	2	2	2	2	2	2	2	2	2	2	2	2	2	2	2	2	2	2	2	2	2	2	2	2
2d Cornets	1	1	1	1	1	1	2	2	1	1	2	2	2	2	2	2	2	2	2	2	2	2	2	2	2	2	2	2
Trumpets, Eb	.	.	.	.	.	.	.	.	.	.	.	.	.	2	4	4	4	4	4	4	4	4	4	4	4	4	4	4
Horns	2	2	2	2	2	2	2	2	1	1	1	1	1	1	1	1	1	1	1	1	2	2	2	2	2	2	2	2
Alto Clarionet	.	.	.	.	.	.	.	.	1	1	1	1	1	1	1	1	1	1	1	1	1	2	2	2	2	2	2	2
Althorns	1	1	2	2	2	2	2	2	2	2	2	2	2	2	2	2	2	2	2	2	2	2	2	2	2	2	2	2
Bassoons	1	1	1	2	2	2	2	2	2	2	2	2	2	2	2	2	2	2	2	2	2	2	2	2	2	2	2	2
Bass Clarionets	.	.	.	.	.	.	.	.	1	1	1	1	1	1	1	1	1	1	1	1	1	1	1	1	1	1	1	1
Tenor Trombones	2	2	2	2	2	2	2	2	2	2	2	2	2	2	2	2	2	2	2	2	2	2	2	2	2	2	2	2
Bass Trombone	1	1	1	1	1	1	1	1	1	1	1	1	1	1	1	1	1	1	1	1	1	1	1	1	1	1	1	1
Euphoniums	1	2	2	2	2	2	2	2	2	2	2	2	2	2	2	2	2	2	2	2	2	2	2	2	2	3	3	3
Eb Bombardons	1	1	1	1	1	1	1	1	1	1	1	1	1	1	1	1	1	1	1	1	1	2	2	2	2	2	2	2
Bb Bombardons	1	1	1	1	1	1	1	1	1	1	1	1	1	1	1	1	1	1	1	1	1	1	1	1	1	1	1	1
Side Drum	1	1	1	1	1	1	1	1	1	1	1	1	1	1	1	1	1	1	1	1	1	1	1	1	1	1	1	1
Bass Drum	.	.	.	.	.	.	.	.	1	1	1	1	1	1	1	1	1	1	1	1	1	1	1	1	1	1	1	1
Cymbals	.	.	.	.	.	.	.	.	1	1	1	1	1	1	1	1	1	1	1	1	1	1	1	1	1	1	1	1
Bb Flügelhorns	.	.	.	.	.	.	.	.	.	.	.	.	.	.	.	.	.	.	.	.	.	2	2	2	2	2	2	2
Bb Trumpets	.	.	.	.	.	.	.	.	.	.	.	.	.	.	.	.	.	.	.	.	.	.	.	2	2	2	2	2
Soprano Saxophone	.	.	.	.	.	.	.	.	.	.	.	.	.	.	.	.	.	.	.	.	.	.	.	.	1	1	1	1
Alto Saxophone	.	.	.	.	.	.	.	.	.	.	.	.	.	.	.	.	.	.	.	.	.	.	.	.	1	1	1	1
Tenor Saxophone	.	.	.	.	.	.	.	.	.	.	.	.	.	.	.	.	.	.	.	.	.	.	.	.	1	1	1	1
Bass Saxophone	.	.	.	.	.	.	.	.	.	.	.	.	.	.	.	.	.	.	.	.	.	.	.	.	1	1	1	1

The above classification is borrowed from "The Military Band" by Lieut. S. C. Griffiths, late Director of Music, Royal Military School of Music (Kneller Hall), England. The omission of a bass drum until a band of 34 is reached, is remarkable, considering that the table was designed to furnish examples of how a band for military requirements should be formed.

The following examples of band formation are: (1) by Sax, the great wind-instrument maker, who was called upon to organize a model band for the French Guides (circa, 1852), (2) Bandmaster Pares of the Republican Guards, Paris, at the present time.

	Sax	Pares
Piccolo	1	1
Flutes	1	4
Oboes	2	3
Bassoons		2
Double Sarrusophone		1
E♭ Clarionets	2	3
B♭ Clarionets	4	17
Bass Clarionets		2
Soprano Saxophone	1	
Alto Saxophones	1	3
Tenor Saxophones	1	3
Baritone or Tenor	1	2
Bass	1	
B♭ Cornets	2	1
C Trumpets		3
E♭ Trumpets	4	3
French Horns	2	4
Trombones	3	4
Sopranino Saxhorn, E♭	2	1
Soprano Saxhorn, B♭	4	3
Alto Saxhorn, E♭	4	3
Baritone Saxhorn, B♭	2	2
Bass Saxhorn, B♭	4	4
Double E♭ Bass	2	1
Double B♭ Bass	2	2
Kettledrums (pair)	1	1
Snare Drum		1
Cymbals		1
Bass Drum		1

The last two examples are much the best of those given. The instrumentation of the Republican Guards, with slight changes, is worthy of acceptance as standard for bands. For concert work, the balance of the organization, 50 per cent reed, is excellent. Family kinship is well maintained throughout and variety of voicing most judicious. Improvements which might be made would be to drop the cornet and sopranino saxhorn, eliminate one C trumpet and one E♭ trumpet as well as one B♭ bass, and in their stead employ two B♭ trumpets, one E♭ bass and one bass saxophone. The two latter would add sonority to the foundation, which in the table appears to need strengthening. Further, the bass saxophone would impart variety in color and link the tone of the double sarrusophone with that of the brass basses. Again, in view of the great sonority of the brass elements, the oboe and bassoon seem to need additions. So large a band should have four oboes and four bassoons. It might be preferable to use but three of each and add a soprano and tenor sarrusophone to take the place of the fourth; by so doing the latter family would be nearly complete. As the band is tabulated the double-reed section appears weak.

The brass band, that is one formed from instruments with cupped mouthpieces and drums only, is in its true sphere as a marching band, where it is preferable to the composite band for such a purpose. There is more of the military spirit about it, its tone being resonant, virile, brilliant. Lack of tone variety, incidental to brass bands as at present formed, could be obviated by use of trumpets and flügelhorns, or soprano saxhorns.

A suggested concert wind-band of sixty-four players, in which the proportion is about two-thirds reed to one-third brass and percussion instruments, offered for the benefit of composers.

Piccolo..............................	1	} OPEN PIPE, side-blown mouth hole.
Flute...............................	2	

Oboe, 1st..........................	2	
Oboe, 2d...........................	2	
Bassoon, 1st.......................	2	
Bassoon, 2d........................	2	
Bassoon, Contra- (with bass).......	1	} DOUBLE-REED FAMILY.
Eb alto Sarrusophone...............	1	
Double Sarrusophone (with bass)....	1	

Eb Clarionet, 1st..................	2	
Eb Clarionet, 2d...................	2	
Bb Clarionet, 1st..................	8	
Bb Clarionet, 2d...................	4	Stopped-pipe principle, straight tube.
Bb Clarionet, 3d...................	4	
Alto Clarionet.....................	2	
Bass Clarionet.....................	2	} SINGLE-REED FAMILY.
Alto Saxophone, Eb.................	1	
Tenor Saxophone, Bb................	1	Open-pipe principle, conical tube.
Bass Saxophone, Eb (with bass).....	1	

Cornets, B♭, 1st or Saxhorn	1 }	Hybrid. Saxhorn preferable.	
Cornets, B♭, 2d or Saxhorn	1 }		
Trumpet, B♭, 1st	1 }	⅔ Cylinder tube, ⅓ conical tube.	INSTRUMENTS HAVING CUP MOUTHPIECES.
Trumpet, B♭, 2d	1		
Trumpet, E♭, 1st	1		
Trumpet, E♭, 2d	1		
French Horns	4	Conical tube.	
B♭, Trombone, 1st	1 }	⅔ Cylinder tube, ⅓ conical tube.	
B♭, Trombone, 2d	1		
F, G or E♭ Trombone	1		
B♭, Tenor Horn	1 }	Conical tube.	
Euphonium or B♭ Bass	1		
E♭ Tuba	2		
BB♭ Bass (Bombardon)	2		
Tympani (pair)	1 }	PERCUSSION.	
Snare drum and traps	1		
Cymbal	1		
Bass Drum	1		
Total	64		

The above, offering sonority in which the reed element predominates, and variety of voicing in family grouping, secures a richness in particular and *ensemble*, outrivaling the orchestra. The "balance," being based on the principle of two-thirds reed as against one-third brass and percussion — the tones of the latter being to color and increase the volume of mass, and not to overbear — would, it is believed, prove exceedingly effective.

Maintaining similar proportions, with here and there deletion to suit varying conditions, the plan permits of subdivision into smaller but yet effective wind-bands.

The following table suggests what might be achieved in the formation of a brass band, numerically limited. For an organization of the above character drums are essential.

Name of Instruments.	Number of Instruments.								
	11	14	15	17	20	22	24	25	26
E♭ cornet or sopranino saxhorn..	1	1	1	2	2	2	2	2	2
B♭ cornet or soprano saxhorn...	1	1	1	1	2	2	2	2	2
B♭ trumpet....................	1	2	2	2	2	3	4	4	4
Flügelhorn...................	1	1	1	1	2	2	2	2	2
Baritones....................	1	1	1	2	2	2	2	2	3
Altos........................	2	3	3	3	3	4	4	4	4
Trombones...................	1	1	2	2	3	3	3	4	4
Bass........................	1	2	2	2	2	2	3	3	3
Drums (brass and snare)........	2	2	2	2	2	2	2	2	2

From the foregoing remarks and presentations in tabular form it will be apparent that band instrumentation is yet in chaotic condition. The remedy lies in the hands of composers. If only they can be brought to consider the wind-band seriously, and, recognizing its potentialities as an art factor, be induced to write works suited to its genus, taking into account its remarkable variety of voicing, its infinite shades of tone color, order will result. He who can and will evolve order from this chaos will earn a niche for himself in the Hall of Fame, and without doubt some consideration tangible and immediately available for mundane comforts.

CHAPTER VI

SINGLE-REED INSTRUMENTS CONSIDERED INDIVIDUALLY

THE CLARIONET, being the most important instrument of the wind-band, naturally comes first in the list for consideration. But, before passing on to its invention, structure and utility, there is something to be said on the manner in which its name is spelled. Chappell, in his "History of Music," treating of the single and double reed principles, remarks, "Horace refers to pipes of his time as being bound with copper or bronze, and as emulating the power of the trumpet. He contrasts them with pipes of more ancient days which were of small bore. The ancient pipes accompanied a chorus, but those of his own time served rather to drown it. This emulation of the power of the trumpet in pipes seems to have suggested the modern name clarionet; for a clarion was a trumpet an octave above the ordinary one, and clarionet is its diminutive." The term "clarion" has always been used in the English language—and in France to this day — to designate a high, shrill trumpet, or instrument of similar character. The Italian term *clarina* has been used for the same purpose, and for that reason many persons have adopted the diminutive *clarinet*, or even *clarinette*, instead of the Anglican form, which, with

49

English-speaking people, should be esteemed the more correct.   The present author has always used the English orthography and does so throughout this work, for the reason stated in the quotation from Chappell's work.

The clarionet is a single-reed instrument, and the principle underlying its vibrations has been known to mankind for very many centuries, far more than the groping mind of the antiquarian can fathom.   Instruments constructed on that principle are known to have been used in ancient Egypt, as representation on a tomb at Memphis shows.   They were also employed by Grecian musicians when celebrating the Pythian games, during which a fight between Apollo and the Python was represented.   The reed used on those occasions was a very stiff one, the object of the musicians being to produce a harsh, strident tone.   An instrument, possessing similar characteristics, but of higher development, was known, later on, as Shawm, Schalm, Schalmuse or Chalumeau, from the Latin *calamus*, a reed, until about three centuries ago.   At that period, 1690, John Christopher Denner, an instrument maker, at Nuremberg, Saxony, experimented with the chalumeau, having in view the improvement of its tone and capabilities.   From those experiments he educed the clarionet, laying the foundation for experiment by subsequent makers and musicians, at whose hands the clarionet as we know it to-day became a fact.

It is an instrument beautiful in quality of tone, affording great facilities to the player, by reason of its mobility

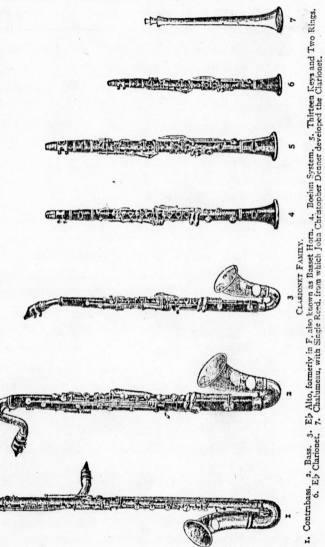

CLARIONET FAMILY.

1. Contrabass. 2. Bass. 3. E♭ Alto, formerly in F. also known as Basset Horn. 4. Boehm System. 5. Thirteen Keys and Two Rings. 6. E♭ Clarionet. 7. Chalumeau, with Single Reed. from which John Christopher Denner developed the Clarionet.

and extended compass of over three and one-half octaves. Yet, great as are its resources, it is imperfect as to intonation and exhibits defects in other directions; facts pointing to need of still higher development. Among the makers who in recent times have contributed to development of the clarionet may be mentioned Sax and Buffet-Crampon of Paris, Albert and Mahillon of Brussels, and Boehm. The system invented by the latter (for the flute but later adapted to the clarionet) did more to remove the trammels which had previously confined its possibilities to a few "keys" ranging on one side of C to A and on the other to E♭. It is now, practically, *omnitonique*, that is, can be played in any key with almost equal ease. Claims are made, however, that the additional side holes, necessitated by the system, have injured its purity of tone. It is an open question whether the increased facilities of digital manipulation compensate for the alleged injury to the tone. For use in the wind-band, and until all instruments are equally free from key trammel, it would seem that clarionets with fifteen keys are equal to all emergencies. The Boehm system gives twenty-one or more keys to the clarionet. Comparison of the facilities this elaborate mechanism affords, with the four-, six- and eight-keyed instruments of former days, shows the enormous advance and superiority of the up-to-date clarionet over those of bygone times.

Not so many years since, clarionets were made from boxwood, varnished or oil finished, otherwise the natural color of the wood remained. The joints and bell were ornamentally mounted with rings of ivory; keys, such as they were, made usually of brass, occasionally of inferior white metal and infrequently of silver. The mouthpiece was made of ebony, but instead of the simple modern ligature, which brings an equal pressure on the reed, the performer bound his reed to it by numerous laps of cord. Clumsy appearing blocks were precursors of the contrivances where now graceful keys snugly fit. Clarionets have been constructed from various materials, such as glass, gutta percha, ivory and even metal. At present wood is most generally employed, *cocus* and *grenadilla* being most in demand for that purpose. Vulcanite, a composite of india rubber and other hardening ingredients, is also used. For hot climates, or those variable and running to extremes, the latter material is the most suitable. It is more impervious to climatic changes than wood and neither checks nor splits.

CLARIONET
MUSIC HOLDER.

The clarinet remained for nearly one hundred and twenty years much as J. C. Denner had left it and, indeed, until the early part of the last century continued to be quite a primitive affair. Limited as was its mechanical capacity, and though its tonal beauties were only half revealed, the instrument had begun to attract the attention of composers as a possible new tone color to add to the meager resources of the orchestra in those days.

About 1810, Ivan Müller (born at Reval, Dec. 3, 1786) effected many improvements, among which he increased the number of keys to thirteen. Müller, who resided at Paris when his improvements were brought forward, was one of the greatest clarionetists of his day. He made a successful concert tour through Europe, the beautiful tone and mechanical facilities of his perfected clarionet attracting attention wherever he performed. His improvements and inventions inaugurated a new era of usefulness for the instrument. Composers vied one with the other, writing solos for and extending its employment in the orchestra. Besides Müller there were others, no doubt, whose achievements are not recorded, who contributed to its development. The increasing importance, as indicated in the scores of composers of the period, marks gradual development and unfolding of its resources. That fact furnishes data sufficient to justify the opinion that others, with Müller, contributed to the improvement of the clarionet. That Weber wrote his magnificent solos for the instrument as early as 1811, Baermann playing them in that year, is ample proof that the technical and tonal resources had not, mushroom-like, sprung to the surface in a night, but rather had developed slowly and surely as an oak tree. Spohr's works may, also, be offered in evidence, his treatment of the clarionet marking a very great advance upon that of Bach. The gradual development of the instrument may be traced during a period of forty-eight years — 1763 to 1811 — in the works of Haydn, Mozart, Beethoven and Weber, and

the date of the addition of each essential key added thus
approximated. The activity of Sax, the elder, born at
Dinant, Belgium, 1791, contributed largely to improvements on the clarionet, flutes, serpents and bassoons.
Those improvements gained for him a medal at the
Industrial Exhibition, 1820, as well as appointment as
Instrument Maker to the Court, and brought him
financial assistance in developing his business. His more
talented son, Antoine Sax, born also at Dinant, 1814,
early displayed remarkable ability as an instrument
maker, and to him must be credited many of the improvements by which wind instruments became of real
practical value as mediums of refined musical expression.
In 1842 he settled at Paris, and two years later made so
fine an exhibit at the French Exhibition as at once to
place him at the head of all manufacturers of wind instruments. He greatly improved the clarionet in bore
and key mechanism. Berlioz, composer and author of
a celebrated treatise on instrumentation, was a warm
admirer of the genius of Sax. From the work referred to,
it may be inferred that the "ring" key on the lower joint
of the clarionet, facilitating the trills,
was added by Sax. This invention
superseded the old side key. At the
time Berlioz wrote his treatise those trills were classed
among others as impossible. Later in the work, writing
on improvements made by Sax, the foregoing trills are
stated as possible, and, besides, mention is made of
the addition of a long key near the mouthpiece. Sax

may have introduced the mechanism by which the trills became practicable, but Berlioz nowhere makes mention of it; on the contrary, he shows explicitly in his table of trills that they were impossible in his time. Sax extended the compass a semitone downwards, thus giving a low E♭ to the clarionet. Why that improvement has not generally been adopted is difficult to say.

Klosé, whose textbook for the clarionet is considered a standard work, adapted the Boehm system to the instrument in the early part of the last century. Modifications, often by suggestion of players, have been successfully made by more recent makers. The present key mechanism appears to meet all technical requirements of the modern score. Additional trill, duplicate and extra ring keys, none of which add new tones, are contrivances attached for the more convenient operation of the original thirteen keys, to facilitate performance of many otherwise very difficult, if not impossible, passages, have come into use since the days of Sax. Credit for them is mainly attributable to Klosé's attempt to adapt the Boehm system for flute to the requirements of the clarionet.

Until about 1800 the smaller forms only of the clarionet were known. In 1805 Dumas, goldsmith to Napoleon I, presented a bass clarionet he had invented, for approval of the Imperial Conservatoire. In 1828 Streitwolf, a manufacturer at Goettingen, constructed the basset horn — an alto clarionet in F. During the following year he also brought forward a contrabass clarionet, the compass of which descended a fourth lower than the bassoon. In 1838 Sax, of Paris, perfected the bass clarionet, employing a tube of greatly increased diameter and augmenting the keys to twenty-two. Homogeneity and more beautiful quality of tone resulted from those improvements. He further constructed a contrabass clarionet in E♭ — an octave lower in pitch than the present E♭ alto clarionet — which descends to a sound in unison with GG of the string bass. Recently a contrabass clarionet in B♭, two octaves lower than the ordinary B♭ clarionet, has been presented. By adding keys to the bell elongation it is said to be possible for the player to reach sounds a fifth lower, thus descending to AAA, or four octaves below *a* in the second space treble clef!

At present the clarionet family, in range of compass, color, mobility of tone, and mechanical facilities, is the most complete amongst wind instruments, affording composers and players scope in expression and execution second only to those of the string group. To furnish an idea of the completeness and range of that family the table on the following page is given. It shows that the tonal range covers the enormous compass of six and one-eighth octaves.

When it is remembered that the majority of compositions for orchestra or band are expressed within a range of five octaves, a better idea of the capacity of the clarionet family will be formed. Nor is extent of

Clarionet Family.	Written.	Effect.
Eb . . . . Clarionet		
C . . . . "		
Bb . . . . "		
A . . . . "		
Alto (Eb) . "		
Bass (Bb) . "		
Contra Bass (Bb) "		8ve bassa.

Some players, especially on Bb Clarionets, extend the compass upwards to C *in alt*.

compass the only point to commend it.   Each clarionet
is distinct from the other in *shades* of tone, a distinction
quite as pronounced as amongst string instruments.   The
ponderous gravity of the contrabass, violoncello-like
effect of the bass clarionet, sympathetic and viola-like
quality of the alto clarionet, beautiful mezzo tints of the
A and B♭ clarionets and crystalline brilliancy of those
in C and E♭, afford ample opportunity for expression in
every degree of emotional force a composer seeks to
depict in the string quartet and quintet.   The possibilities of the clarionet family are great and have never yet
been done full justice to.   Although some of the great
masters have written for the individual instruments, no
continued effort has ever been seriously made to show
off the characters of all in concerted action.

The pitch of the normal sound of a wind instrument is
dependent on the length of its main tube.   For instance,
the speaking tube of a concert flute, about two feet in
length, gives [musical notation] ; the C clarionet, of similar length,
emits a sound [musical notation] a sixth lower, that is [musical notation].
That difference involves two principles.

In the pipe organ there is employed a class of pipes
plugged at one end, from which sound issues at a lip
situated a short distance from the opening, through
which the wind is injected with force sufficient to pass
the point of emission and onward to the plug, where it is
diverted, doubles back on itself, retraversing the pipe
until reaching the lip, where it finds egress.   Those pipes,
termed "stopped pipes," emit sounds, the pitch of which

is equal with that of "open pipes" of twice their length.
The doubling backwards of the air column within the tube
explains why such a result is obtained. The clarionet
acts on this "stopped-pipe" principle. All other reed
instruments, including the oboe, bassoon, saxophone
and sarrusophone, have conical tubes and act on the
"open-pipe" principle. The clarionet has a cylindrical
tube.

The peculiarity affects the *timbre* or tone color of the
clarionet, imparting to it that veiled character, especially
in the low and medium registers, at once so noticeable and
pleasing. Further, it exercises an influence on the fingering, for the reason that its harmonics do not occur in
sequence similar with those of other instruments mentioned, or of those having cupped mouthpieces. On the
flute, oboe, saxophone and sarrusophone, fingering of any
given note in a lower octave is the same as that in the
octave above, the upper sound being produced by increased pressure of wind and slight contraction of the
lips, for which reason they are sometimes termed octave
instruments. The clarionet, as a stopped pipe, does not
give an octave when the fingers lie in position for its
lower sounds and attempt is made to produce a higher
sound. On the contrary it gives a twelfth
by opening the harmonic key, numbered
12 on charts of fingering. It may here be noted that
the key just referred to, as well as the long side key,
fulfills its chief function when employed to facilitate
the emission of harmonics. They create "nodes," as do

the fingers when lightly touching certain points on violin strings to produce harmonics. Without the twelfth key it would be impossible to pass to the upper register of the clarionet. More knowledge of acoustics pertaining to his special instrument, than at present obtains, would benefit the instrumentalist. Every one concedes such knowledge as necessary to the instrument maker, but it is surprising how few musicians appreciate the advantages to be derived from the study and its practical application to "fingering." To learn fingering by rote is not sufficient. He should know how and why exceptions can be made. Thus equipped he may overcome difficulties inseparable from his particular instrument with more ease than is possible from knowledge gained from the average textbook.

Harmonics of the clarionet are said to follow each other in the ratio of 1, 3, 5, 7, whereas on all other wind instruments they occur in the ratio of 1, 2, 3, 4, 5, 6, 7, 8, etc. According to that theory the harmonics of the clarionet, from its fundamental sound, would occur in the following sequence:

From this statement it is obvious that the next sound above the lowest possible with the same fingering — excepting with the addition of the twelfth key for the purpose already noted — is the twelfth. Reference to any chart of clarionet fingering will show that the succession of first with twelfth obtains throughout the chalumeau and clarion registers.

the upper sounds with harmonic or nodal key open.

As noted in a previous chapter, Chappell does not admit the existence of any harmonic on the clarionet, excepting the third, ♯♪ that is, the first twelfth and a twelfth higher: 𝄞 ● . In this he takes issue with Helmholtz and his disciples, on the ground that to open a key changes the fundamental note, apparently overlooking the nodal point obtained by opening the twelfth key, which, as every clarionet player is aware, covers a very small hole. Many clarionet players when fingering b′, third line, have occasionally been surprised by a sound other than expected. The sound, which in its crude state resembles the much dreaded "quaack," is really no other than the fifth in the series of harmonics. That and other sounds similarly produced can be cultivated, not only to facilitate fingering, but also to add variety to tone color at points where desired in a solo.

The clarionet has four registers, entitled *chalumeau*, from *calamus*, a reed, extending from e to f′, a ninth above; the second, or *throat*, from g′ to b′♭, a minor third (this is really the break between the first and third registers); the third, or *clarion*, from b′ to c‴, a ninth above, and the *high* from d‴ upwards. It is in satisfactorily connecting those registers that much of the art of clarionet playing lies.   Each one, being as distinct in character as are the chest, head and falsetto registers of the human voice, requires quite as much practice to master its manipulation.

The peculiarity of the harmonics of the clarionet distinguishes it from all other instruments.   There is no instrument used in the band at once more useful by reason of its compass and easy manipulation, nor more desirable on account of its exquisite tone color and the readiness with which the same blends with either double-reed, brass, string or vocal families of the tone world.   Each register has a distinctive tone color, capable of being fused into a chain of sounds great in variety, rich in texture, uniting the gravity of the low sounds of the viola to the plaintiveness of the oboe, the clear utterance of the trumpet and the crystalline brilliancy of the flute.   Although the clarionet is an almost incomparable medium for musical expression, it is not without defects of intonation.   Inherent defects are noticeable in the series of twelfths above the chalumeau register, particularly so in the following:

In the first series the upper sounds have a tendency to flatness; in the second the variation is complex, the lower sounds inclining to sharpness, with the reverse in the upper, excepting the upper b′ natural, which, on many

SCALE FOR CLARIONET WITH THIRTEEN KEYS

Indications, ●, hole closed; O, open; ■, thumb hole closed; □, same open; numerals refer to keys.

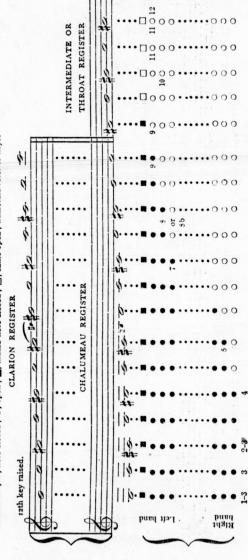

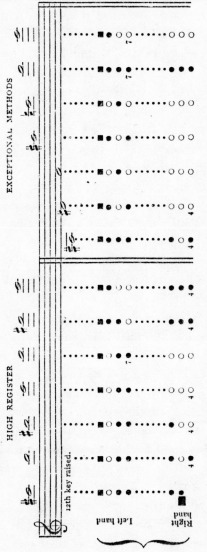

HIGH REGISTER

EXCEPTIONAL METHODS

12th key raised.

Left hand

Right hand

The 15 keyed clarionet, so called, has a duplicate 8th key, which may be operated by the 1st finger of the right hand for 〳 instead of the usual 8th key. The other is on the lower joint, operated upon by the 1st key, which 〳 acts as a lever. It is used to facilitate 〳 instead of key 2.

The 13th key is harmonic and employed to improve tune and 〳 emission of some dull sounds.

The keys are numbered according to relative position of holes they cover.

instruments, is too sharp.   The throat notes are not only weaker in quality, but also are more susceptible in the matter of pitch, owing to their proximity to the mouth-piece, from which may be inferred that the influence of rising temperature, caused by the steady ingress of warm breath, is more readily and earlier felt in the part of the instruments wherein those notes lie.   The notes of the high register, beginning with c''' sharp, require to be very carefully watched; the high e''' and f''' are particularly prone to flatness.   But as from c''' upwards each note may be fingered in two or more ways, it is possible for the performer, by judicious selection, to overcome these radical defects so as to leave little to be desired.   There is no defect so great on a well-constructed clarionet that it may not be overcome by the player who will sedulously and logically study the instrument.

Next to the flute the clarionet is the most flexible of all wind instruments.   While better adapted to *legato* in execution, the *staccato* is by no means foreign to its possibilities.   Extreme rapidity of *staccato*, single, double and triple tonguing, easily possible on flute, cornet, etc., is next to impossible on the clarionet.   Sections and short phrases of *staccato* notes, single or iterated, may be accomplished at considerable speed, and continuous passages at a moderate gait.   Flowing scale and *arpeggio* passages, and those in mixed or varied articulation, have no speed limit and are better adapted to the clarionet, besides being more conducive to development of its tone.

Purity of tone is much dependent on the "reed," the

relation of which to the clarionet is similar to the vocal cords in the human larynx for production of sound. It is the vibratory medium, and its beats, or oscillations, determine in great extent the quality of tone. If the reed be stiff the tone will be harsh, and its production entail much labor on the player. If it be too soft the tone will

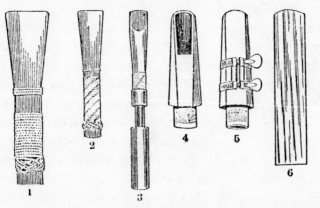

REEDS AND MOUTHPIECES.

1. Bassoon and Sarrusophone. 2. Cor anglaise. 3. Oboe. 4. Mouthpiece for Clarionet, or Saxophone showing face or "lay." 5. Same with reed held in position by "ligature." This mouthpiece differs in size for various Clarionets and Saxophones, as also does 6, showing form of reed for those instruments.

be thin; the reedy quality will dominate that pipe-like character noticeable in the efforts of fine players. Further, on either it becomes almost impossible to control the intonation, especially in the upper clarion and high registers. The reed most to be preferred, as best adapted for all purposes, is one of medium strength, having a straight, evenly disposed, close grain, elastic and progressively opaque toward its feather edge.

The mouthpiece exercises great influence on the tone of a clarionet. Its form is thus described in Grove's "Dictionary of Music and Musicians": "The mouthpiece is a conical stopper, flattened on one side to form the table for the reed, and thinned to a chisel edge on the other for convenience to the lips. The cylinder bore passes about two-thirds up the inside, and there terminates in a hemispherical end. From this bore a lateral orifice is cut in the table, about an inch long and half as wide, which is closed in playing by the thin edge of the reed. The table on which the reed lies instead of being flat is purposely curved backwards towards the point, so as to leave a gap or slip the thickness of a sixpence between the end of the mouthpiece and the point of the reed. It is on the vibration of the reed against this curved table that the sound of the instrument depends. The curved table is of considerable importance."

The reed and mouthpiece should be regarded as of the highest importance and great care bestowed on their selection and preservation. When purchasing a new mouthpiece for an old clarionet the diameter of the bore of both should conform to a hair's breadth; regard should also be paid to the "lay" of the mouthpiece, otherwise the merits of a good body may be sacrificed to a defective head, as is often the case in other things besides clarionets.

The instrument is susceptible to change of temperature, its pitch being raised by heat or lowered by cold. Once it has absorbed heat or cold it retains the same much longer than do brass instruments. Its tendencies must be carefully watched by the player and any deviation corrected at once. The "throat," coming first in contact with the player's breath, naturally warms and sharpens more rapidly than the lower parts. This fact accounts for the flat pitch of the low e and middle b' and adjacent sounds noticeable amongst careless players. To counteract this defect requires great exertion, increased pressure on the reed and mouthpiece being necessary, until an equal temperature has been established throughout the tube.

THE SAXOPHONE is a single-reed instrument made of brass and has a conical tube, its mouthpiece being similar to that of the clarionet. It is of comparatively modern invention and originated from the fertile brain of Sax. The ophicleide — a now nearly obsolete brass instrument having keys and cupped mouthpiece — is supposed to have suggested the saxophone. The discovery of Mons. Sax lay in substitution of the reed mouthpiece for the cupped mouthpiece and certain modifications in diameter and form of tube, as well as key arrangement and equipment, which now mark the difference between the saxophone and its prototype.

The family consists of B♭ soprano, E♭ alto, B♭ tenor or baritone and E♭ baritone or bass, having a collective compass of about four and a quarter octaves, an extent of sounds sufficient to meet requirements of composition and satisfy demands of players. Works finding their expression in the medium range, rather than the ex-

tremely low or high, are always more acceptable by the
public, and in such works saxophones are particularly
expressive.

As the harmonics of the saxophone are identical with
those of the oboe and flute, its fingering exhibits many
points of similarity.   It differs materially from the clarionet in each of those respects.   However, players on the
three instruments last referred to find little difficulty
acquiring mastery of the former.   Flute and oboe players
require to adapt themselves to change of mouthpiece
only, fingering being nearly the same, and the clarionetist,
already accustomed to the reed and form of mouthpiece,
experiences little difficulty with the fingering, as that of
the second octave of the saxophone is identical with the
clarion register of the clarionet, the lower octave on the
saxophone being fingered as though he were reading an
octave higher than the expressed notes.

Scale range, or compass, of each of the family extends
through about two and a quarter octaves.   In the hands
of good players it may be extended a third higher, but, it
should be remarked, all notes in the upper fifth of the
range are apt to be fitful in quality of tone and intonation.

Saxophones have a quality of tone color peculiar to
themselves, seeming to unite the tone of reed instruments
with that of the brass, with a tendency to the nasal and
somewhat string-like.   It is a composite quality, and
as produced by an efficient player possesses a vague
charm that carries the hearer into the region of doubt as
to the true nature of the instrument; for, in the medium

register, the tone decidedly resembles the amalgamated effect of clarionet, cor anglais and violoncello, whereas, in other parts it suggests a combination of a clarionet with some brass instrument.   This singularity, adding, as it

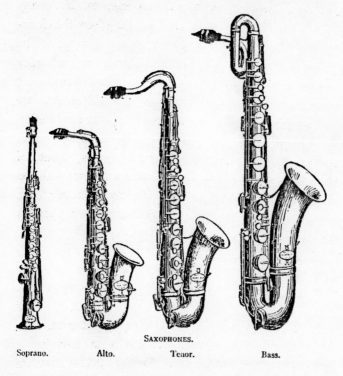

SAXOPHONES.

Soprano.   Alto.   Tenor.   Bass.

does, a rich composite voice of great breadth to the wind-band, makes the saxophone a most valuable instrument and very desirable in any well-constituted organization.

Similarly with all single-reed instruments it is better adapted to *legato* rather than to *staccato* articulation.   **In**

the former its possibilities nearly equal those of the clarionet in scale passages and arpeggio. But (and this applies
progressively to the whole family) the breadth of its tone
appears to indicate movements of a cantabile nature as
the best sphere in which its characteristics may be displayed. There, and in sustained harmonies, the family
chiefly excels. Its rich tonal coloring, to say nothing
of sonority, is such as to arrest attention of lovers of fine
musical effect and point to the conclusion that the saxophone possesses a most necessary and, it may be said,
indispensable voice to add to and fuse with others of the
wind-band. This quality has long been recognized by
bandmasters of France and Belgium, where saxophones
have a permanent place in band instrumentation. In
America, England, and many continental European
countries, their usefulness is being slowly admitted.
Teutonic conservatism is, no doubt, commendable; but
sometimes, as in this instance, it retards the· wheels
of progress.

CHAPTER VII

DOUBLE-REED INSTRUMENTS

THE OBOE (It.), hautboy or hautbois (Fr.), belongs to the double-reed conical-tube family of wind instruments, in which it occupies the position of soprano to the cor anglais and bassoon respectively. Its harmonics are those common to all open pipes, occurring in the ratio of 1, 2, 3, 4, 5, 6, 7, etc.

Next to the flute it is probably one of the oldest of wind instruments, being known in a primitive form to Egyptians, Phœnicians, Greeks, Romans and all nations of antiquity. The Egyptian collection at the British Museum contains a small pipe, eight and three-quarters inches long, into which is inserted at one end a split straw, forming the reed. The principle of the reed corresponds precisely with the modern oboe reed, and the instrument, as a whole, fits well with the description of the "Gingras" of the old Greek writers. The Phœnicians called the same kind of pipes "Gingroi," and employed them (as also the Carians) for lamentations

1. ANCIENT BASSOON.
2. OLD FORM OF OBOE.

for the dead.   From this fact the instrument is supposed
to be of Asiatic origin.   A well-executed picture of a
Roman youth, holding two conical-shaped instruments
fitted with double reeds and pierced with holes, as are
oboes of the present day, is to be seen in the British
Museum.   This, the oldest pictorial representation of
the oboe extant, proves that the Romans were acquainted
with the oboe.

Mersennus (born 1588), a French writer, and the author
of several erudite works on music and musical instruments, in one of which ("De Instrumentis Harmonicis")
he gives descriptions of all instruments then in use.
Among others he describes the "hautboy" as a "treble
instrument invented by the French, and also the instruments used in concentus with it, namely, the Bassoon,
Bombardt, Fagot, Courtant and Cervelt." He gives
illustrations of a treble, tenor and bass hautboy.   The
latter was five feet long and of conical shape.   Its appearance is peculiar from the fact that three of the eleven
holes with which it is pierced are covered by a box surrounding the instrument a little above the center.   Those
holes are reached by keys, part of which are seen in the
illustration to be protruding from the box which is liber-
ally perforated with holes to permit the sound to escape.
The treble and tenor hautboys, exhibited by the author,
being very similar in appearance with the Roman hautboy above referred to, raise a doubt as to the soundness
of his claim that the instrument was "invented by the
French."   The hautboy was formerly held in esteem as

the highest-toned wood instrument. Hence its name "*haut bois*," high wood.

The hautboy was used in England as far back as the reign of Edward III, 1327 to 1377 A.D. It was there known as the "Waeght," three of which were included in the instrumentation of the King's private band. The name had its origin in the fact that the "Castle Waight," or Watchman, was required to carry and play a rude kind of hautboy at stated hours of the night, hence, "Wayghtes," "Waights" or "Waits."

The oboe has been used as an orchestral instrument since about 1720. Bach (1685-1750) employs two kinds of oboes in his "Passion Music," the "oboe d'amore," a sweet-toned variety, and "oboe da caccia," which was similar to the cor anglais of modern times. Beethoven was very partial to the oboe, employing it frequently in his scores. In his "Pastoral" and "Eroica" symphonies he uses it as a solo instrument and assigns a delicious obbligato to it in his opera "Fidelio." Haydn, Handel, Mozart, Mendelssohn, and in fact all composers since their times, have used it freely. Rossini evinced his liking for the oboe in "The Italians in Algiers," "William Tell" and others of his operas. As a rule the great writers have used it to express contentment or sorrow, or to depict pastoral effects. That it has higher possibilities is evidenced in the many brilliant solos written for it by practical oboists.

The oboe tone is of plaintive, pastoral color, but in the hands of a good player is peculiarly sweet, and in the low and medium registers somewhat resembles the human voice. It requires judicious treatment, otherwise rebels, displaying waywardness in faulty intonation, disagreeable "quaacks" and tones rivaling the chanter of a bagpipe. Well played it is most sympathetic, responding readily to the mood and desires of the player, at times blithe and gay, at others sad and doleful. Capable of the utterance of refined emotions and brilliant flights it can never become impressively noble or grand. It is the feminine sex amongst wind instruments, quite as coquettish and variable as womankind in general. The tone possesses penetrating qualities, so much so that two oboes afford ample color for an orchestra of sixty or a wind-band of about forty. In the softer passages their tones are clearly distinguishable, while in louder efforts their absence would be felt, although not so obvious under such circumstances.

The oboe has a range of compass from   to . All styles of articulation are possible from extreme *legato* to *puntato*, quick or slow. Octave and *arpeggio* passages and rapidity of execution are limited only by ability of the player. A good ear and sensitive embouchure are among the chief essentials to mastery of the instrument. The fingering is very similar to that of the flute and saxophone, and, being an octave instrument, the adaptation of the Boehm system affords every possible key facility for overcoming any difficulties to be encountered in modern writing.

For over one hundred years the oboe has been considered indispensable in a well-organized orchestra, and for many years similarly appreciated as of great use in wind-bands. That such is the case is quite natural and a sequence to its employment in former days, when it was used as the leading instrument in bands attached to regiments, as well on the continent of Europe as in England, where, as has been mentioned, it was used in the King's band in the early part of the fourteenth century.

THE COR ANGLAIS is the alto of the oboe, sounds a fifth lower, has a double reed, conical tube and sequence of harmonics exactly like the latter. Its tube is longer and wider in diameter, and in it the bell, vase-like in the oboe, is of somewhat globular shape. It has a range of compass similar with that of the oboe, with which its fingering is identical. The tone is dreamy and pathetic, approaching somewhat the quality of the human voice, for which reason it is named *vox humana* in Italy. Except for special effects it is rarely used in orchestras or wind-bands, which is a pity.

The instrument is said to have been invented by Joseph Ferlandis of Bergamo, 1760, but the truth of that statement is doubtful. He may have improved one of the members of the family, from which, as has been shown, the oboe was descended. In its early days in Austria the tube was bent at its upper part, slanting inward towards the mouth from its greater length; in France the bend was at the middle. That form was adopted for convenience in playing, but objections to it, as injuriously affecting the tone, and difficulty in creating the bore to avoid a certain interference with and deflection of the air column, led to its being constructed as a linear tube by one Brood. The form of the bell exercises an influence on the tone of the instrument by first allowing the air column to expand and next by again compressing it before final emission. The key arrangement is identical with that of the oboe in all respects, and the Boehm system has been applied to it with equally good results.

As its early history is bound up with that of the oboe and bassoon, it is unnecessary to make further reference to it.

THE BASSOON belongs to the double-reed family and forms the natural bass to the oboe. It has a very extensive compass, beginning with [♪] and ascending to [♪]. All chromatic semi- tones within its compass of three octaves are possible. Through the lower fifth of its scale rapid passages are difficult, each note being produced by sliding the thumb of the left hand from key to key. Trills are impossible in that register, and in the high range of the instrument are often very difficult. The bassoon is written for in bass and tenor clefs, the latter to avoid use of ledger lines in the high range.

The great extent of its compass, combined with modern key facilities, makes the bassoon one of the most useful of wind instruments either in orchestra or band. It is

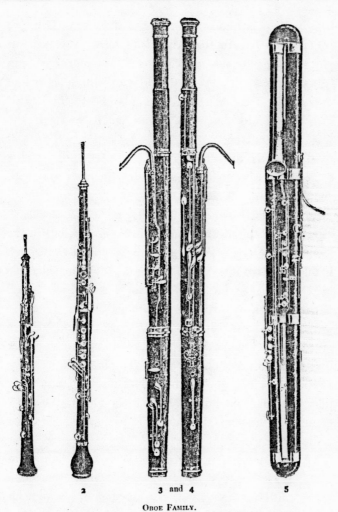

OBOE FAMILY.

1. Oboe. 2. Cor anglais. 3 and 4. Showing front and back of Bassoon.
5. Adler Contrabassoon.

possible to play in all tonalities, but those of C, G, D, F, Bb, Eb and Ab are the easiest and most generally employed. Legato passages, connected and in *arpeggio*, can be performed with great rapidity, excepting as before noted; but the staccato is less adapted to the instrument and more difficult of acquirement, owing to the breadth of its reed.

Its tone is of sympathetic character, approaching somewhat that of the violoncello, and blends readily with the flute, clarionet, French horn, oboe, all string instruments and the voice. The tendency inclines to the nasal, especially in the medium and upper registers, but in the low scale its tone is more broad and sonorous. Though highly effective in sympathetic and serious melodies, as in " Robert le Diable," and extremely useful in sustained harmonies, there is a vein of jocularity in its temperament. This characteristic has been brought out in grotesque and comical situations by several of the great masters, who have not hesitated to employ it as the clown of the orchestra, notably in Beethoven's "Pastoral Symphony," Mendelssohn's "Midsummer Night's Dream," Gounod's "Funeral March of a Marionette," and other compositions.

The bassoon has been recognized as possessing great usefulness subsequent only to Handel's time, that composer, with one exception, scoring for it, as did his predecessors, to supplement or strengthen the voice and string bass parts. Handel's one exception is to be found in his oratorio "Saul," where he employs it with fine effect in the scene of Saul and the Witch of Endor.   Lully, the French composer and director of the king's music (1634), is said to have been the first to introduce the bassoon in the orchestra.   Now most important parts are assigned to it, and from being the drudge of a century or so ago, it has become one of the most useful reed instruments in orchestras and wind-bands pretending to be well balanced.

Besides the bassoon ordinarily used there are two other varieties — the *bassoon-quinte* and the *contra-bassoon*. The former is smaller and voiced a fifth higher than the B♭ bassoon, and the latter, much larger, voiced one octave lower.   Thus, there exists a complete family of double-reed instruments, having conical tubes, whose harmonics are as those of the "open pipe," already referred to.   The family is as follows:

Oboe...................... Soprano.
Cor Anglais.................Contralto.
Bassoon-quinte..............Tenor.
B♭ Bassoon.................Baritone and Bass.
Contrabassoon..............Bass and Contra.

Introduction of this complete family would benefit the concert wind-band.   It would enrich the harmony and impart a tone color impossible to obtain from any other instruments.   The contrabassoon has a powerful tone, well adapted to that of the brass basses, subduing their harshness and rounding out their volume.

Afranio de Ferrara, a Catholic priest (1540), is the reputed inventor of the bassoon.   By reason of its resemblance to a bundle of sticks, he named it "Fagotto," and it is still so named in Italy. Mersennus, writing about a hundred years later, makes a distinction between the fagotto and the bassoon, the former being analogous with the bassoon-quinte, and the latter including the larger varieties. Afranio may have improved the bassoon, but that he invented it is doubtful. According to Stainer and Barrett, "There is reason to believe that the bassoon is of Eastern origin, introduced in western Europe in the twelfth century, and that it is an improvement of the drone-pipe of the bagpipe. The Egyptian word for a pipe of deep tone, and for the drone of the bagpipe, is, according to E. W. Lane ('Modern Egyptians'), *Zummarah-bi-soan*, and the manner in which the word *Buzaine, Buisine* is used in medieval manuscripts, shows the possible connection with this origin." Again, the *Bombos* of the Greeks and *Bombardt* of the middle ages are understood at the present time to have been similar in tonal character with the modern bassoon. Otherwise, in its equipment of keys, improved bore and general appearance it is much superior to the bassoons represented by the quaint engravings to be found in histories of music, illustrative of those used in the days of Afranio and Lully and probably earlier times.

THE SARRUSOPHONE, invented by the French bandmaster, Sarrus, of the second empire, after whom it is named, is a double-reed instrument, and its harmonics are identical with those of the oboe and bassoon groups.

It is fingered the same as the oboe and saxophone and possesses a similar compass, that is, two and one-fifth octaves. The sarrusophone, made of brass, has a conical tube, several times curved about itself. Its reed is similar to that of the bassoon, fits on to a "crook," as is the case with the latter, but differs in size according to the varying requirements of each member of its family.

The idea of the inventor appears to have been to provide wind-bands with instruments of double-reed tonal characteristics, wherein the sonority should be greater than that of oboe and bassoon. In point of sonority he succeeded, but failed in his effort to obtain a tone of equal purity with those named. The quality is more vague, and while it does not lack in roundness, seems to suggest a loss of the free vibrations so noticeable with other double-reed instruments. In that sense it is a hybrid, but none the less valuable as an adjunct to wind-band instrumentation, where it might be employed to supplement the oboes and bassoons, without, in large bands, replacing them.

The sarrusophone family consists of: (1) B♭ soprano, (2) E♭ alto, (3) B♭ tenor, (4) B♭ baritone, (5) B♭ bass and (6) E♭ contrabass, and has a collective compass of five and a quarter octaves. The E♭ alto is a beautifully voiced instrument, worthy a place in the concert wind-band, but is rarely employed. The contrabass is more frequently found, but not so often as its merits demand. Its tone is of great sonority and depth, and the colorable vibration of its double reed blends splendidly with the brass basses, than which it is more facile of utterance and agility.

In point of mechanical possibilities, what has been said of the oboe and bassoon applies to this family. It is essentially *legato* in its characteristics and quite at home in scale and *arpeggio* passages.

CHAPTER VIII

OPEN PIPE WITH SIDE-BLOWN MOUTH HOLE

THE FLUTE is, and for many ages has been, so useful and popular that a sketch of its antecedents will not here be considered out of place.

The antiquity of the flute is unquestionable. According to Dr. Jahn in his " Archæology," Jubal, who, Genesis iv, 21, is termed "father of all such as handle the harp and the organ," was the first to cause the pipe or fife to utter sweet, musical sounds. At first sight no authority may appear for such an assertion, as the above reference is all that is made to that antediluvian musician. The term "organ " is from the Hebrew word *ugahb*, derived from the verb *agahb*, to blow, indicating that it represented a wind instrument. Horne and others, with Dr. Jahn, held the belief that the "organ" referred to was simply a kind of flute or pipe, at first used singly and later on in varying lengths and dimensions joined together, as in the well-known Pan's Pipes. The instrument in its primitive form is found in use among Orientals of the present day, and is of such antiquity that ancient writers knew not who was its inventor. Jubal may or may not have invented the flute, but that he was a musician of some note in the land of Nod, or thereabouts, is confirmed by the practice of Arabians and Persians of the present day. Cain was head of the family from whom Jubal was sixth in descent, and in Arabia and Persia the generic term applied to musicians is *Kayne*, or descendants from Cain.

Exodus xv, 20, furnishes the next reference to the pipe, fife or flute principle, and after that none other until the days of Samuel. The interim was filled with the noisy blasts of trumpets and cries of victory. The "pipe" referred to in 1 Samuel x, 5, is said to have been made from either reed, bone or wood. In the Jewish canon the term is *hhalil*, a verbal from *hhaáll*, to pierce, to bore through; in the Septuagint (Greek) it is *aulos*, a flute. From this allusion it is evident that the Jews had profited musically from their association with the Egyptians, amongst whom the flute in various forms was a favorite instrument. This carries our consideration of flute history by a backward step into the land of the Pharaohs.

There can be little doubt that the effect produced by wind blowing across the edge of broken reeds first drew attention to their possible musical qualities and led to their utilization in the form of pipes. The discovery that the height and depth of sounds evolved by blowing at right angles across the end of reeds was dependent upon their length, was one that would speedily be made once the first effect had been observed. It was a case of cause and effect and from it came the acoustic law of inverse ratio. The fashioning of those reeds into the form of Pan's Pipes, so called, was a result as natural to occur as the combination of metal reeds in our times, in the mouth harmonica. The basic principle of each is the single reed. Pan's Pipes were well known to the Hebrews and Grecians, who unquestionably acquired their theoretical and practical knowledge from the Egyptians. Daniel iii, 5, 10, 15, is the only place in which the above is referred to in Holy Writ. The Hebrew word is *mashrogiytha*, derived from the word *sharag*, to hiss or whistle. In the Septuagint it is rendered *syrinx*, the Greek name for Pan's Pipes, while in our version it is translated as flute. By many it is still held to refer to the double flute of the kind still used in Arabia. This instrument consists of two tubes, bound together and blown into at the same time, one of which, perforated with four holes, is for playing the melody, and the other, very much longer, for playing a drone bass. Double and single pipes, as well as the flute proper, were in use among the Egyptians in the beginning of the fourth dynasty. The pyramids of Memphis and Gizeh furnish illustrations of musical organizations, in which pipes (termed *mam*) and side-blown flutes (*seba* or *sebi*) were both used. Pipes and flutes of great length were employed. In some of the illustrations engraved from the originals in tombs and pyramids the above instruments are so long as to give rise to the supposition that they were an octave lower in pitch than concert flutes of the present day. The side-blown flute was used in the worship of the Egyptian god Serapis. Other flutes and pipes were employed indiscriminately in religious service, revelry, war and peaceful pleasures. Some pipes used by Egyptian musicians had a stiff mouthpiece. From them the flageolet is descended.

The Grecians copied their musical instruments from the Egyptians, but endeavored to hide the source of their knowledge. Thus, discovery of the pipe, attributed to Osiris in the older mythology of Egypt, is in the Grecian myth credited to Pan by Virgil, Mercury by Pindar, and to Marsyas and Silenus by Athenæus. Pipes and flutes were known in Greece under the generic title of *aulos*, and later amongst the Romans as *tibia* and *fistula*.

The materials employed by the ancients for construction of flutes and pipes were of various kinds, such as lotus wood, laurel, pinewood, boxwood, elder wood, ivory, different sorts of reeds, leg bones of animals and of large birds, as the eagle, vulture and kite. Horns of animals and also metal were used to make the "bell" ends of certain pipes. In Greece, the names assigned to pipes indicated their use, such as Spondauloi, for supplicating the gods; Chorauloi, for accompanying choruses; Choriki, for accompanying choral dancing; Dactylic pipes, for a sort of dance in common time; Hippophorboi, for horse keepers, and others for travelers, shepherds and so on.

Chappell, source of much of the foregoing, says, "pipes were sometimes named after the country or nation from which they were derived, as Alexandrian, Tuscan, Thebian, Scythian, Phœnician, Lybian, Arabian, which were very long pipes, and Phrygian or Berecynthian. The Lybian was a true flute, blown at the side; a Plagiaulos.

It was made of lotus, and so was distinct from the horse-keeper's flute, which was also attributed to Lybia. The Scythian were eagles' or vultures' legs, and the Thebian were made from the thigh bone of a fawn and were covered with metal. The length of the Arabian pipes was proverbial, and a man of whose tongue there seemed to be no end was called an Arabian piper."

The Monaulos was, according to Sophocles, derived from Egypt. It was a single pipe, blown at the end, made from reed, was punctured with finger holes and known as the Shepherd's pipe of Tityrinus. On account of the sweetness of its tone it was employed at weddings.

The Plagiaulos, or side-blown flute, so named from the fact of being held laterally while playing, was also known as the Photinx among the ancient Greeks. The Tibia Obliqua of the Romans was the same kind of instrument.

An interesting account of flutes or pipes used among the natives of Peru is given by Garcilasso de la Vega in the "Royal Commentaries of Peru." The author narrates, "in music they arrived to a certain harmony, in which the Indians of Colla did more particularly excel, having been the inventors of a certain pipe made of canes glued together, every one of which, having a different note of higher and lower, in the manner of organs, made a pleasing music by the dissonancy of sounds, the treble, tenor and bass exactly corresponding and answering to each other; with these pipes they often play in concert and made tolerable music, though they wanted the quavers, semiquavers, aires and many voices, which

perfect the harmony amongst us.   They had also other
pipes, which were flutes with four or five stops, like the
pipes of the shepherds; with these they played not in
concert, but singly, and tuned them to sonnets, which
they composed in meter, the subject of which was love
and the passions which arise from the favors or dis-
pleasures of a mistress.   These musicians are Indians,
trained up in that art for divertisement of the Incas and
the Caracas, who were his nobles, which, as rustic and
barbarous as it was, was not common, but acquired with
great industry and study."   From which we learn that
pipes and flutes, similar in form and purpose to those
used by the Egyptians, Grecians and Romans, were also
used by the semicivilized inhabitants of America at the
time of the Spanish conquest.   That the Aztecs of Mexico
had them is well known, and discoveries amid the ruins
of Yucatan show that the former people of that interesting country were acquainted with flutes and pipes.   In
fact it is now certain that the Indians, so called, from
north to south on the American continent, were familiar
with pipes in some form.   This opens up an interesting
anthropological inquiry outside the province of this
sketch.

Until about a century ago the term flute was applied
to all single pipes.   The flageolet was *flauto dritto*, *flûte à
bec* (beaked flute) or English flute, the side-blown *flauto
traverso* being known as the German flute.   The name
flute is derived from *fluta*, Latin for a lamprey, or small
eel, caught in Sicilian seas, having seven holes on its body

corresponding with the holes on the front of the flute. In former days it was customary to play quartets and trios on flutes, they being constructed in lengths suitable to produce soprano, alto, tenor and bass tones. The largest flute used at present is the concert or grand flute, with compass descending to c', and sometimes b, below the treble staff, but in earlier times the bass flute could descend a fifth lower, to f. Specimens of flute quartets are still extant.

From the foregoing it is obvious that the flute, in some one or more of its various forms, has been a favorite instrument from very remote times. It has been devoted to all purposes, sacred and secular, and has been identified with the history of all nations. Yet, until very recently, its higher possibilities were practically unknown. While the ancients devoted much thought to beautifying the exterior, the moderns have given attention to development of its interior. Experiments with the bore and key mechanism, from the one-keyed flute of the early part of the eighteenth century, have been in steady progress, culminating in that marvel of acoustical and mechanical ingenuity found in the Boehm system, by which it has reached a state of musical perfection and utility far beyond the most exalted ideals of the ancients. Among those who have devoted their attention to development of the flute may be mentioned Denner, Phillibert, Stanesby, Quantz, Gordon, Nicholson and Boehm.

The flute is to-day one of the easiest of all wind instruments to blow, but with the Grecians it was not so, for

TABLE OF FINGERING FOR FLUTE OR PICCOLO, ORDINARY SYSTEM

DIATONIC SOUNDS   CHROMATIC SOUNDS   For flute descending to C

Indications, ●, hole closed; □, key open; ◼, key closed.

with them it was required to protect the cheeks and lips of the player by leathern bands, in form somewhat like a halter.   Phorbeion and Capistrum were the terms applied respectively by the Greeks and Latins to the bandage which served to support the facial muscles in the effort to produce high sounds.   Alcibiades drove the flute out of fashion among high-born Athenians by insisting that to play it disfigured the beauty of the mouth.   A sculpture in the British museum indicates that some clever person arose equal to the emergency, and by invention of a mouthpiece, fitted into the mouth hole, restored the flute to favor.   Necessity no longer exists for bandaging the cheeks, neither do modern players, male or female, fear that performance on the flute will impair the beauty of their lips.

From the days of Cavalière, Peri and Monteverde, the flute has been included in "scores" of opera, oratorio, symphony, concerto and all kinds of instrumental music. Its usefulness, great flexibility, sweet tone, extended compass of at least three octaves, and great popularity, no doubt accounts for the liberal manner in which it has been written for by eminent composers, as well as those of less attainments.

Up to a certain point the technique of flute playing is easily acquired, a reason accounting for the numerous flautists in embryo to be found on every hand and altitude from basement to attic and midway in the drawing room.   In the hands of a good player it is possible to surmount the greatest technical difficulties and, thanks to the Boehm system, in any key. It has a tone of much beauty, which, lacking in breadth and dramatic intensity, is suited to passages of refined brilliancy and pathos. The concert flute is best known to amateurs and the dilettanti, but others are used in the orchestra and wind-band for extending the range upwards beyond limits possible to the former. Of such are the E♭ and F flutes, so called, and the C and E♭ piccolos. Incidentally it may be remarked that the E♭ flute is really D♭, the F flute E♭ and the E♭ piccolo is D♭. The pitch of a piccolo is an octave higher than a flute of similar denomination.

No orchestral instrument, excepting the violin, can compare with the flute in its capabilities for execution. *Legato* or *staccato*, *arpeggio* or connected passages, trills, near-by intervals or extended skips, single, double, triple or quadruple iterations of notes may be played with the most remarkable degree of rapidity and precision. Improvement in intonation inaugurated by Gordon (1739) and perfected by Boehm (1802), extending to diameter of the tube and readjustment of its finger holes, ranks the flute among the most accurate of musical instruments and gives it an importance previously unknown.

Though there is little authority, if any, for the statement, the application of the movable headpiece for tuning has been ascribed to Quantz. An old engraving shows an Arabian double flute (date uncertain), the drone pipe in which is divided, manifestly for changing its pitch at pleasure.

The harmonics of the flute are similar in sequence with

those of all string instruments, as well as wind instruments constructed on the open-pipe principle. Thus the same fingering employed for any one of its lower notes will be found to give a rising series of tones, (1) the octave, (2) fifth, (3) double octave, (4) seventeenth and so on, by merely forcing the wind more strongly into the mouth hole. This harmonic aspect of flute playing is little understood by flute players, and yet it is one worthy of attention; because it adds variety to tone quality, and also, affords opportunities for simplifying the fingering of many otherwise difficult passages.

TABLE OF NOTATION AND EFFECTS.

FLUTES, PICCOLOS AND SINGLE AND DOUBLE REED INSTRUMENTS.

The notation of Flutes and Piccolos in
all keys is expressed ....
In key of C, the Flute sounds as written,
Piccolo an octave higher.

EFFECT. — Eb Flute and Piccolo (8ve).
"   Both misnamed, their pitch
        is Db................
"   F flute also misnamed, is
        really Eb ....
The playable compass in alt falls some-
what short of the examples.

Oboe, cor anglais, Saxophone and
Sarrusophone (excepting Contra Sarrusophone), all written for ....

EFFECT. — Oboe as written,
"   Cor Anglais, in F, sounds..

"   Soprano Bb Saxophone and
"   " Bb Sarrusophone,
            sound.........

"   Tenor Bb Saxophone and
"   " Bb Sarrusophone,
            sound ....

"   Baritone Eb Saxophone and
"   " Eb Sarrusophone,
            sound.........

"   Bass Sarrusophone, in Bb..

TABLE OF NOTATION AND EFFECTS.—*Continued.*

EFFECT.—Contra Sarrusophone, in E♭

8ve bassa.

" Bassoon and Contra Bassoon are written for alike, at concert pitch. The latter sounds 8ve below.

Notation for all Clarionets excepting Contra Bass is expressed alike, thus as for C Clarionet......................

EFFECT.—Clarionet in B♭ ....

" " " E♭ ....

" " " E♭ Alto ......

" " " B♭ Bass......

" " " Contra Bass in B♭
" " " Written.........

8ve bassa.

This last instrument is voiced one octave below the Bass Clarionet. Its additional key mechanism enables production of notes down to A A A as above, actual sounds being........................

8ve bassa.

CHAPTER IX

BRASS INSTRUMENTS WITH CUPPED MOUTHPIECE

THE FRENCH HORN, of all brass, cupped-mouthpiece instruments, may justly claim precedence for musical beauty of tone, rich color, dynamic flexibility and sympathetic vibrancy, but which, by reason of its great length, narrowness of tube and smallness of mouthpiece, is more difficult to play.

Prior to the beginning of the eighteenth century, a horn, named *cor de chasse*, having its tubes arranged in spiral convolutions similar with those of the French horn of to-day, was used in France, hence its name; but, it may be observed, *cor d'harmonie* is the title assigned to it in that country. The tone of the hunting horn, being powerful and brilliant, was well adapted to produce signals of the chase. Those qualities precluded its use among the orchestral resources of the period. Subjected to modification, it was later admitted to the orchestra, but not without strenuous opposition by stickers for musical purity, as being "coarse and vulgar." Once it had been introduced the French horn speedily won its way into all the leading orchestras of Europe. This may be seen from the statement that between the date (1720) of its first employment in England by the opera band of the Haymarket, in Handel's "Radamists," and 1770 —

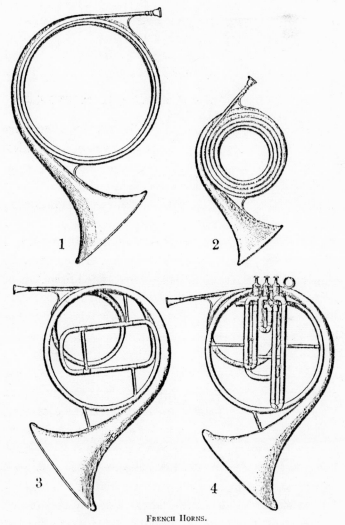

FRENCH HORNS.

1 and 2. Hunting Horns. 3. Hand Horn. 4. French Horn with three pistons.

when Hampl, the Dresden horn player, discovered that by inserting the hand into its bell, notes required to fill gaps in the fundamental series of open tones could be produced — it had won recognition from all composers of eminence.

According to Kappey, in "Military Music," "the horn was introduced into the orchestra of the Imperial Opera at Vienna, from 1712 to 1740, after which it seems that its use was discontinued for a time," a period which the same author assigns as over fifty years, when it was again employed as the *Waldhorn*. The statement is not borne out by facts. Fourteen years after the horn is said to have been discontinued (1754), Johann Werner, second horn player in the above opera orchestra, brought forward an invention "by which the longer crook could be inserted into the center of the horn." He further states, "the records of the Royal Theater of Dresden show that there were two horns in the orchestra in 1711." The fact is that the date at which the horn was first admitted to the orchestra is uncertain and its period of desuetude more or less a myth. The introduction of the horn into French orchestras is attributed to F. J. Gossec (1757), thirty-seven years later than its advent in England. J. S. Bach (1685-1759) included parts for horns in many of his scores, as also did Handel (1685-1759) and Haydn (1732-1809). The foregoing and other composers "scored" continuously for horn, during the period which, Kappey states, it fell into disuse. Either he is wrong, or composers, regardless of the circumstance, "scored" with an eye to the future.

For about sixty years after its first introduction into the orchestra, horn players had only the sounds of the open tube, in ratio of 1, 2, 3, 4, 5, 6, 7 and so on to 19, at their disposal. At that time it was customary to subdue the then coarse tone of the oboe by inserting a pad of cotton wool in its bell. Hampl, above referred to, presuming that the same substance would be similarly effective in the horn, experimented with it and was surprised to find it raise the pitch of his instrument a semitone. "Struck with the result," writes W. H. Stone, "he employed his hand instead of the pad, and discovered the first original method by which the intervals between the harmonic series of open sounds could be partially bridged over." The notes thus produced were termed "hand notes" and the instrument itself became known as the "Hand horn." In France those sounds were designated *sons etouffés* — stuffed or muffled sounds — because their quality as "closed" sounds differed much from the open sounds. This discovery, greatly extending its usefulness, was speedily adopted by players and composers. It filled out the scale of the harmonic skeleton, increasing the possibilities in combinations of sounds for purposes of harmony, and enabled composers so to write their horn parts that when weird or mysterious effects were required they employed "hand notes," or, in more frank and joyous mood, availed themselves of the "open sounds."

In the early days of the horn in the orchestra it was necessary, as with clarionets to-day, for a horn player to be equipped with instruments in different keys. But this, cumbrous and expensive as it must have been for the player, was an advance artistically upon the practice immediately preceding, when all horns being made in the key of F, they could be used only when a composition chanced to be written in a key wherein some of their open sounds could be employed. In the beginning of the eighteenth century this clumsy and ineffective system was overcome. The horn was reduced in length from twelve to about seven and a half feet, and differential "crooks," varying in length from one and a half to ten and a half feet, were made, thus enabling the player, by addition of one or the other to his instrument, to place it, practically, in any key within the compass of an octave.

The following are the "open sounds," or harmonics, previously referred to, some of which require considerable "humoring" to make them correspond with our scale of equal temperament.

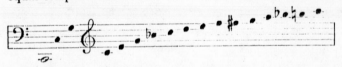

The following scale exhibits the improvement effected by Hampl's discovery, the "closed sounds" being indicated by black notes, and the "open sounds" by whole notes.

Next, the intermediate notes are shown:

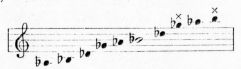

The notes marked x can be obtained open, but their intonation, as also that of the whole note B♭, is more certain by stopping.

For all closed notes but three the bell is entirely "stopped" by the hand. For two of the three the bell is about two-thirds stopped; for the third sound, it is one-half stopped.

The method of "stopping" is "to draw the fingers together, by causing the index and fourth fingers to meet at their tips in front of the second and third, the thumb reaching into the triangle thus formed. In this way the hand forms a sort of wedge, closing it almost entirely when pushed forward sufficiently, or to be withdrawn one-half or two-thirds or altogether, leaving proportionately more space for egress of the air column, as occasion demands. When the hand is not thus in use the bell of the instrument is allowed to rest upon the open palm, the hand being well drawn back, so as not to come in conflict with the air column on its passage outwards."

Valves were applied to the horn in 1820, the originator being Blümel, an oboe player. This improvement has also been ascribed to Stoezel or Stölzel. W. H. Stone ignores the claim set up for either, and shows that the "rotary" or "swivel" valve has its first authentic record in patents taken out by John Shaw, 1824 and 1838. Whether Blümel, Stölzel or Shaw invented the valve is immaterial to the present consideration. The contrivance was but a germ that, in the hands of more skillful men of later date, developed into a thing of great utility. Antoine Sax early recognized the latent possibilities in the crude valve of his predecessors and lent his energy and great mechanical ingenuity to its development. To him has been ascribed the application of the "piston" valve to the horn. In Austria and Germany the piston attachment has never become as popular as in France, England and some other countries. The action of the rotary valve is said to be more readily responsive to the touch of a player's fingers than is the piston valve, which may explain the preference exhibited by Austrian and German musicians. On the other hand it is claimed for pistons that they are more reliable, and much less likely to get out of order than is the more delicate and complicated mechanism of the rotary valve.

The function of valves or pistons, as applied to brass instruments in general, is too well known to need further comment in this place. Yet, owing to the fact that the sounds most used on the French horn are the high ones of the harmonic series, it is advisable to point out that for all practical purposes two valves are sufficient. Equipped with them an extensive chromatic scale may be obtained. The only notes missing which might be had by use of a third valve are 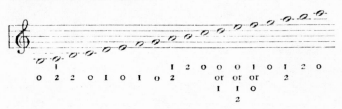. Here "stopping" with the left hand would be necessary. The low F♯ is practically worthless with the combination of valves 1, 2 and 3.

The following scales will show the possibilities of a two-valve French horn.

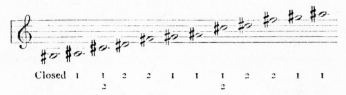

Chromatic notes are fingered as follows:

Besides which, owing to the close sequence of harmonics generated by each change of valve, are many exceptional fingerings. A word of explanation is here necessary. Presuming the main tube of a horn to generate a given series of sounds, each valve when pressed down, opening an air way into additional and successively greater lengths of tube, will naturally change the total length of the instrument, thus generating a new series of sounds lower in each case, but having the same ratio as those of the open tube. For instance, referring to the first example given, it is seen that the upper harmonics begin with the seventh, thus:

The second valve lowers the pitch of the entire instrument a semitone, the first valve a full tone, and first and second combined, a tone and one-half. Transposing the above as indicated, we obtain for each the following series of upper harmonics:

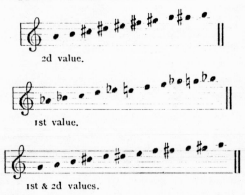

2d value.

1st value.

1st & 2d values.

A comparison of these fingerings with those first given will prove interesting and instructive. From the foregoing it will be apparent that the valves may be used to take the place of crooks, presuming the player should wish to use his instrument as a hand horn, which may become necessary in old compositions where composers require closed sounds, the two valves proving as effective as three crooks. Combinations resulting from addition of a third valve would give the effect of three other crooks, thus affording him facilities as great as — and in some respects greater than — those enjoyed by the hand-horn player with six crooks. It should be remarked that the third-valve combinations are apt to be out of tune for structural reasons apparently impossible to overcome. For reasons above stated and implied it is a question if the addition of the third valve is of value to the French horn, in proportion to its added weight and cost.

Valve horns met with much opposition when first introduced, but improvements that have taken place in construction of wind instruments in general during the past sixty years have almost obliterated the animus. Formerly empiricism obtained, now science directs the operations of instrument makers, and it is questionable if the poorest creations of to-day do not excel the most perfect of those of the beginning of the last century.

The beauty of tone, compass and facilities for execution combined in the horn make it most desirable for wind-band or orchestra. Its tonal character is distinctive, being sympathetic, diffusive and readily blending with those of other instruments, to which it imparts a rich-ness and variety of color not obtainable from any other.

The sounds produced are an octave lower than the written notes. A cornet in B♭ playing from the same part as written for a horn in B♭, high, would sound an octave higher, because its normal tube is only about half the length required for the latter. There is this excep-tion, the fundamental sound of the horn, always noted in the bass clef, stands at its true pitch when the horn is in C, and approximately so when in any other key. For some reason, explainable only by the word "convenience," parts for horns have invariably been noted in the treble clef from their second open sound upwards, consequently an octave higher than the true sounds.

Again, when writing for four horns it is usual to consider the higher pair as first and third, and the lower as second and fourth. As the pair first mentioned deals with the upper sounds, players, as a rule, use a mouthpiece having a somewhat smaller cup and face than do the second pair. Especially is this the case with the fourth horn player, who has to produce the lowest sounds and occasionally the fundamental. The use of a larger mouthpiece permits the lips to vibrate more freely, or in more relaxed manner, than does the smaller one; thus the low sounds are more easily enunciated.

Horn parts being written in various keys, from B♭ high to B♭ low, the following table is given to show the difference between the noted and actual sounds:

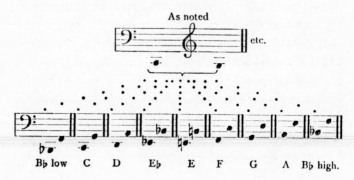

As noted
B♭ low   C   D   E♭   E   F   G   A   B♭ high.

Finally, Berlioz gives the following as "the compass
of horn with three pistons, in a mixed key like the key
of E♭."

Note the apparent difference between the last note, F,
of the bass, and first, F♯, of the treble series. It illus-
trates the previous remarks as to the singular manner in
which horn parts are plotted.

THE TRUMPET is an instrument with long, narrow tube,
cylindrical in two-thirds and conical in one-third of its
length. It has harmonics incidental to all open pipes,
but which, by reason of the small diameter of its tube, are
more clearly voiced than in the cornet and other instruments of similar bore. "The quality of tone of the trumpet is noble and brilliant; it suits with warlike ideas,
with cries of fury and vengeance, as with songs of triumph;
it lends itself to the expression of all energetic, lofty and
grand sentiments and to the majority of tragic accents.
It may even figure in a jocund piece, provided the joy

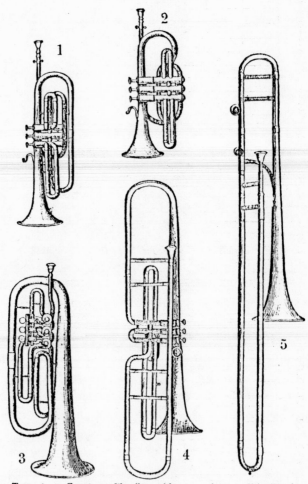

1. Trumpet. 2. Cornet. 3. Flügelhorn with rotary valves. 4. Valve Trombone.
5. Slide Trombone.

FINGERING FOR TRUMPET AND FRENCH HORN (the latter with hand or two, or three valves).

1. The notes to F♯ below are always written in the treble clef in practice.
2. The notes written sound an octave lower on the French-horn than on the trumpet.
3. Pedal C of French Horn is always written in Bass clef as above.
4. B shows that the hand is to be inserted in the bell, manipulating it to obtain notes as called for, on the "hand horn."
5. * Comparison of fingering on two or three valve horn will show exceptional methods.

assume a character of impulse or of pomp and grandeur."
— *Berlioz*.

Formerly the orchestra trumpet did not have valves;
later, a slide, similar to that of the trombone, was introduced, and still later pistons were adopted. When
the valveless trumpet was used it was necessary to
employ "shanks" or crooks — lengthening pieces — in
order to change its pitch and thus meet the exigencies of
the composition   Open sounds only were then the rule,
as none other, similar with the cavalry trumpet, could
be produced. To meet the requirements of key changes,
the player had to carry with him shanks and crooks
sufficient to enable him to put his trumpet in B♭, C, D,
E♭, E natural, F, G and so on, as occasion demanded.
The slide trumpet obviated, to some extent, the need
of lengthening pieces, for by simply changing the position of the slide, the effect derived from them was the
same.   Further, the slide enabled the player to obtain a
full chromatic scale from or to its seventh or lowest
position, as is the case with the slide trombone. The
introduction of pistons did away with the slide, and now
any but the valve trumpet is rarely employed in orchestra
and never in the wind-band.

Trumpets are now made in C, B♭, E♭ and F. To
obviate necessity for the player owning the last two, a
crook, equal to production of a full tone lower, is furnished with the F trumpet by makers. Others, also,
may be had if required. Parts written for the old-style
trumpet still exist. In the following table the actual

and nominal sounds, from the third open sound of the
tube, are indicated.

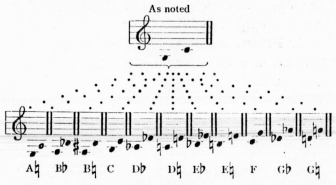

The trumpet in C utters its written notes at actual
pitch and therein differs from the horn, the tube of which
is twice as long, and it sounds an octave lower than those
of the former.

Trumpets in B♭ should be used more generally in
wind-bands than they are, if not to entirely supplant the
cornet, at least to impart a rich and vibrant tone color,
that in its compass cannot be produced from any other
brass wind instrument. It should also be supported
by trumpets in E♭ or F, to connect with the trombones,
which furnish its natural tenor and bass.

The trumpet, in some form or other, is of great antiquity. The Chinese, whose authentic history dates
back 2000 B.C., have always included the trumpet among
their musical instruments. One was shaped like an
enormous cigar, another resembled our common fish horn,
and still another is said to have had a "slide." The most

quaint appearing is a trumpet having two odd bulbous enlargements of the tube, at a slight distance one from the other, but nearer the mouthpiece than to the bell, which is outspreading, as with ours.

The Hindoos have a variety of trumpets, and in certain districts, as is customary in China, employ their stentorian tones to frighten the evil spirit from casting his shadow over the sun or moon, whenever one or the other is going into eclipse. They, too, like the Jews, "Blow up the trumpet in the new moon."

Travelers inform us that trumpets are to be found in nearly every country on the globe. Sometimes a conch shell is used, as among the islanders of the South Pacific, in South America, where Indians on the Orinoco had a trumpet seven feet long of other material, and in Mexico. In the Congo region of Africa, side-blown ivory trumpets are used, and in Ashantee the natives adorn their war trumpets with human jawbones. In New Zealand the Maoris carve a representation of female lips around the mouthpiece of their trumpets.

The Jews were very partial to trumpets, of which they had three kinds: the *Keren*, formed of a ram's horn; *Shophar*, a very long variety turned up at the extremity, and *Chatzozerah*, a straight silver trumpet, used chiefly for sacerdotal purposes. The keren caused the walls of Jericho to totter and the shophar was used for rallying the tribes. Josephus gives the length of the *Chatzozerah* as 21 inches, and is authority for the statement that in the days of Solomon 200,000 of them were in use.

It is probable that Moses acquired the straight trumpet from Egypt, as it is now known to have existed in that country in his day. Further, the Egyptians had trumpets of various patterns, some measuring a few inches, others upwards of four feet, but all terminating with a dilated bell. Under the titles *salpinx* and *kerux* trumpets were used by the Grecians. The Romans named any short, straight trumpet of metal or other material *buccina;* their cavalry trumpet, made from bronze, was known as *lituus;* besides which they had the *tuba* and *cornu*, the latter curved and quite large.

In medieval times trumpets were the prerogative of kings, princes and nobles, and could be used only by them or in their service. They were used for fanfares and signals and in bands of musicians attached to courts or other regal or semiregal establishments of the nobility.

From the foregoing it is apparent that trumpets have an universal and interesting past; they date almost from earliest recorded history and have been associated with events that changed the destinies of nations. They have marched in line with the progress of civilization, and their perfection has been attained correlatively with our own present standing in that scale.

THE TROMBONE is kin to the trumpet, to which, in its several varieties, it forms the natural alto, tenor and bass. It is cylindrical in two-thirds of its length and conical in one-third, which ends in a "bell." Its tubing is of narrow diameter, varying, of course, in different members

of the family, and its harmonics are those of the open
tube. Of all brass instruments none are so perfect as
the slide trombone. Each note in its chromatic range
of two and a fifth octaves may be produced accurately
in tune, by manipulation of the. slide, directed by ad-
monitions of a good ear. Discrepancies of intonation
incidental to valve instruments have no existence on the
slide trombone, but, by reason of its simple structure, it,
like the violin, affords vast opportunities for discordant
utterances in the hands of an inefficient player.

The slide operates on a fixed inner tube, which it
lengthens, by being pushed outwards, to stated "positions," at the distance of a semitone apart, until the interval of a diminished fifth below the sound of its first
"position" is reached, which, for the B♭ tenor trombone,
would be [♪]. Four descending semitones, at
least an   octave lower, may be voiced, but
the gap between these "fundamental" or "pedal" notes
and their octaves cannot be filled, for reasons already
given. Each movement of the slide is termed a "position," of which there are seven, including the first, or
"closed position."

Trombones have been made in many different keys,
from the E♭ alto to the E♭ bass trombone, an octave
lower than the former. Those most commonly used are
the B♭ tenor, and F, G or E♭ bass; the E♭ alto rarely.
By reason of the great length of tubing in bass trombones,
they are fitted with a swivel handle, attached to the upper
"stay" of the slide, to enable players to reach the lower

KEY BUGLE TRIBE.

1. Serpent progenitor of Key Bugles. 2. Kent or Key Bugle. 3. Bass Bugle or Klappenhorn. 4. Ophicleide. 5. Modern Infantry Bugle, with, 6, valve attachment, by which it may be played as is the cornet.

positions.   Mouthpieces vary in size with each member
of the family, being progressively larger from E♭ alto to
E♭ bass, a fact indicating differences in quality, volume
and flexibility of utterance; the former being high and
agile, the latter ponderous and grave, but all characterized by vibrant resonance of their sounds.

The following table indicates the compass and positions of the trombones named.

Positions — Closed or 1st.   2nd, 3rd, 4th, 5th, 6th, and 7th by
successive lengthenings of the slide.

The notes marked * are all too flat in practice, and those corresponding in other positions are similarly so.

It may be remarked that Sax, among his many other
inventions and improvements, added a piston valve to
the B♭ tenor trombone, which, under control of a finger

of the left hand of the player, could be used for trills, or
to lower its pitch a semitone, when pressed down to open
the air way.   Further, it could be employed to enable
the player to fill, chromatically, the gap existing between
fundamental sounds (E♭ to B♮) and their octaves, already
referred to, the pedals of the first four positions continuing the compass down to G, one octave below G, first line
bass.

The slide trombone has always been held in high esteem
by composers for the dramatic possibilities of its tone,
which in turn becomes awe inspiring, terrible, exulting,
jubilant and even sympathetic.   It possesses all the virile
and energizing appeal of the trumpet, amplified by increase of diameter.   For those reasons its employment
in wind-bands is most desirable, not only, as is usual, in
pairs of B♭ tenors, but also by addition of one or other of
the more voluminous, if less agile, bass trombones.   Employed in that manner, and where trumpets (not cornets)
form part of the instrumentation, it would be possible
to organize a quartet having the true trumpet ring from
soprano to bass.   Thus:

1. B♭ Soprano Trumpet.
2. E♭ (Alto) Trumpet.
3. B♭ Tenor Trombone.
4. F, G or E♭ Bass Trombone.

For special effects, tone color, or enrichment of harmony, such a quartet is invaluable to the wind-band.

As will be apparent, the slide trombone is not adapted
for performance of *legato* passages, the *staccato* style of

articulation being best adapted to its character. Its construction, especially so in the bass trombones, is suggestive of distinct, dignified utterance, rather than rapidity of speech. Consequently, all solo efforts should be directed towards maintenance of its individual tone character.

Historically the trombone covers similar ground with the trumpet, for, indeed, it is a trumpet of amplified dimensions. The principle was known to Assyrians, Egyptians, Hebrews, Grecians and Romans, which latter used a large curved trumpet (*cornu*), its bore suggesting the diameter of the trombone, and, as has been shown, when treating directly of the trumpet, it was largely utilized by the ancients. It is interesting to note that the Romans had instruments structurally similar to modern slide trombones. During excavations at Pompeii, in the reign of George III, instruments of the kind were recovered from the ruins of that unfortunate city, and presented to his majesty by their finders.

Valve or piston trombones are, as the name implies, trombones with those auxiliaries attached, and much that has been said in respect to the valve trumpet applies to them. Pistons enable the player to lengthen the main tube of his instrument and in effect fulfill the objective purposes of the slide. Discrepancies of intonation incidental to all valve instruments are in evidence, requiring equal skill and judgment to attemper and overcome. But limitation as to *legato*, present in the slide trombone, is removed and, in that respect, as well as in facility for making the trill, the valve trombone is on a plane of· equality with all other instruments similarly equipped.

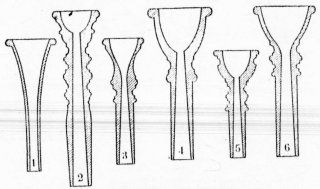

INTERIOR FORM OF MOUTHPIECES FOR BRASS INSTRUMENTS.
1. French Horn.   2. Trumpet.   3. Flügelhorn or Saxhorn.   4. Trombone.
5. Cornet.   6. Tuba (Bass).

THE CORNET stands in a class by itself among cupped-mouthpiece brass instruments.   It has a conical tube of narrow diameter, like its ancestor the old post horn.   Its mouthpiece differs in form of its cup from those of the French horn and trumpet, as it does also in style of tube, and for those reasons acquires a distinctive quality of tone color.   It occupies a position between the trumpet and soprano members of the saxhorn family, without exhibiting the noble clarity of the former, or the sonorous sweetness of the other, for which reasons it may be considered a hybrid instrument.

It is in the "open-pipe" class, and has the harmonic sequence of that form, but, similarly with all other soprano cupped-mouthpiece instruments with a tube of narrow diameter, its first open sound readily available is an octave higher than the fundamental sound of the series, the same being difficult to produce.

Cornets most generally used in wind-bands are in B♭ and E♭. In the orchestra the cornet in A is used, which lowering is effected by means of a shank or set piece inserted in the body of a B♭ cornet. When such an addition is made, the slides controlled by first, second and third valves must be drawn successively longer in order to establish conditions of pitch in each essential to the new key of the instrument. In former days cornets were made in other keys, but have fallen into disuse. Cornets are written for in the treble clef, and the first open sound of each is nominally C, the actual pitch of which is the key name of the instrument, thus:

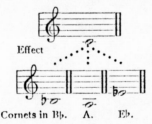

Cornets in B♭.   A.   E♭.

By pressing the pistons down successively in order of 2, 1, 3, 2 and 3, 1 and 3, 1, 2 and 3, the scale may be caused to descend to ⟦ ⟧, from which it may ascend through all chromatic semitones to but, for reasons already given, the sounds produced by combinations of valves in the lower register are out of tune.

All varieties of phrasing, excepting the *arpeggio* and extended skips, are possible, and even the exceptions, in movements of moderate rapidity, may be played. Rapid iteration of notes, by single, double, triple or quadruple tonguing, are a somewhat flamboyant feature of cornet playing. Trills are possible on nearly every note of the compass.

Volume of tone may be reduced to proportions of an echo, by insertion of a pear-shaped contrivance, termed a "mute," into the bell of a cornet. A mute with piston arrangement is sometimes attached to a cornet; the effect is the same, but its ungainly appearance and cumbrousness are against its general adoption.

B♭ cornets are employed in the wind-band as first, second and third, but, for the last two, the flügelhorn, or B♭ soprano saxhorn, having wider tubing and vibrating more freely in the lower (and, in fact, the upper) register, would produce better results, by broadening the tones for accompanying parts.

The name cornet would appear to indicate a similarity of construction and purpose with an instrument of the same designation used in medieval times. Such is not the case, for the ancient cornet was a reed instrument, much used in England and originally made of horn. From it is descended the cor anglais, or corno inglese, a member of the oboe group.

The cornet has never been taken seriously by great writers, who have always ignored attempts to intrude it among the recognized resources of symphony and operatic orchestras. The following excerpts furnish an idea of the estimation in which it is held by intelligent writers:

"The habit which exists nowadays of hearing in ball orchestras, melodies devoid of all originality and distinction executed on this instrument, together with the character of its quality of tone, which has neither the nobleness of the horn, nor the loftiness of the trumpet, renders the introduction of the cornet-à-pistons into the high melodial style a matter of great difficulty." — *Berlioz.*

"The cornet has obtained a most prominent place, and being of easier manipulation than the trumpet and flügelhorn, it has pushed into the background these two instruments, both of which have a better tone color and character." — *Kappey.*

"It has been brought into discredit by being unwisely used in some orchestras as a substitute for its parent the trumpet, with the grandeur of which it cannot compare." — *Stainer* and *Barrett.*

"The cornet is a true bastard." — *Mahan.*

"Its tone is, however, much more coarse and vulgar" (than the trumpet), "and is far more fit for the performance of dance music . . . than for classical compositions." — *Prout.*

"This instrument is the *gamin de Paris* of the orchestra, more at home in dance halls and café concerts than in grand opera or symphonies, whence it would be well that it should disappear." — *Lavignac.*

Many similar opinions as to the musical merit of the

cornet could be gathered, but the foregoing are sufficient to indicate the disesteem in general in which it is held by the *cognoscenti*.   Consequently, in any efforts made, tending to the artistic betterment of the wind-band, the question of perpetuation or elimination should be gravely discussed in all its bearings.

SAXHORNS.   This family, comprising seven members, originated in the labor of Sax, hence its name.   It consists of:

1. Eb Sopranino Saxhorn.
2. Bb Soprano Saxhorn.
3. Eb Alto Saxhorn.
4. Bb Baritone Saxhorn.
5. Bb Bass Saxhorn.
6. Eb Bass Saxhorn.
7. BBb Bass Saxhorn.

They have conical tubes, with harmonics incidental to all open pipes, and the usual complement of pistons. Sax made them originally in upright form, but later changed some of them to be played horizontally, as is the cornet.   Berlioz remarks of them, "Their tone is round, pure, full, equal, resounding, and of a perfect homogeneousness through all the extent of the scale," results which could be obtained only by mathematical nicety of formation of their tubes, and conformation and adaptation of a mouthpiece to each best fitted to assist in producing a gradually increasing breadth of tone throughout the whole family.

In France the Eb sopranino and Bb soprano are largely used to take parts which with us are assigned to Eb and

CHART OF FINGERING FOR PISTON INSTRUMENTS IN BASS CLEF, WITH POSITIONS OF SLIDE TROMBONES. IN Bb, F, G, AND Eb.

Bb Bass Euphonium and Valve Trombones in Bb.

Note. BBb Bass 8ve lower than here written.

Eb Bass with three valves.

Positions of Slide Trombones in

This chart is based on the acoustic harmonic series of sounds, on the open tube or pipe principle. Harmonic 7ths are omitted, as being too flat for use. Comparison of the columns will show different methods of fingering on piston instruments, as well as on "positions" on slide trombones.

Black notes are the enharmonics of the white ones. They are written differently, but are fingered the same, and sound as do the white notes.

TABLE OF FINGERING FOR BRASS-CUPPED MOUTHPIECE INSTRUMENTS READING IN THE TREBLE CLEF, AS CORNET, FLÜGELHORN AND SAXHORNS.

	(note)	(note)	(note)	(note)	(note)	(note)	(note)	(note)	(note)	(note)	(note)	(note)
H.	2-3 or o	2 or 1-3	1 or 1-2-3	1-2 or 3	2-3	o or 1-3	2 or 1-2-3	1	o or 1-2 or 3	2 or 2-3	1 or 1-3	1-2 or 3 or 1-2-3
M.	2-3 or o	2 or 1-3	1 or 1-2-3	1-2 or 3	2-3	o or 1-3	2 or 1-2-3	1	1-2 or 3	2-3	1-3	1-2-3
L.	o	2	1	1-2 or 3	2-3	1-3	1-2-3					

H signifies high octave. M, medium octave. L, low octave.

B♭ cornets, a preference that evinces judiciousness and superiority of musical taste. "The mouthpiece of the soprano saxhorn is deep from the lip to the throat, approximating in this respect somewhat to the mouthpiece of the horn. This gives the mellowness of tone which this instrument possesses. Its large bore gives a fullness and richness to the notes below which cannot be had by the cornet. Monsieur Parès, bandmaster of the Garde Républicaine of Paris, himself a cornet player of high order, says that the low notes come out much more easily and with better effect on the soprano saxhorn than on the cornet. Furthermore, he calls it the singer *par excellence* of the band." — *Mahan.* In Belgium, also, the B♭ saxhorn is used in preference to the cornet. The sopranino possesses the quality of brilliancy devoid of the shrillness associated with the tones of the E♭ cornet.

The five remaining members of the family are known to us simply as E♭ alto, B♭ baritone, B♭ bass, E♭ bass (or tuba) and BB♭ bass (or bombardon). The baritone and B♭ bass have the same pitch, difference in diameter of tubing accounting for the broader quality of tone of the latter. The euphonium is a modification of the B♭ bass saxhorn, that is, when retaining the proportions introduced some forty years or so since by Mr. Phasey of London. With the majority of players the two names are interchangeable and applied indiscriminately. The B♭ baritone is called B♭ althorn in England.

Sax also introduced the saxotrombas, which had tone

quality more resembling the trumpet group, occasioned by narrower diameter of tubing. Some modern makers approach that form in their altos, baritones and Bb basses, with a result that is far from satisfactory when played with other instruments of the true form.

Application of four, five and even six pistons is by no means immediately modern. Sax experimented with all and made instruments accordingly. We hear in these days of fifth valves, compensating pistons, transpository valves and many other contrivances, as though they were new inventions of this, that or the other firm, but Sax antedated them; his genius embraced the whole field, even to the circular forms of the deeper bass instruments, as shown in his sax-tubas.

Before Sax entered the field as an instrument maker, wind-bands, such as they were, presented a weird aspect, and produced a most wonderfully complex, often inharmonious not to say discordant agglomeration of sound. The elements entering into their formation were all awry, no uniformity of dimensions or forms, no scientific adaptability of mouthpiece; some instruments had keys, others valves of various kinds, imperfect in construction and ill-fitting; relationship by groups of instruments had not been thought of, in fact no such thing as kinship existed, and the wind-band was a heterogeneous mass of badly assorted sound mediums, such as the key bugle, ophicleide, serpent and Russian horn, all calculated for effect of "sound and fury, signifying nothing but noise" and that in volumes immeasurable.

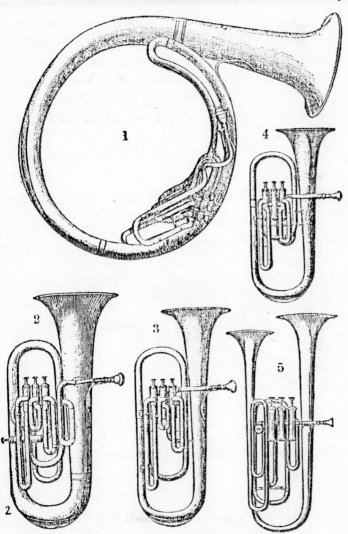

1. Circular (helicon) bass constructed in E♭, also in BB♭. 2. Euphonium or B♭ bass.
3. Baritone in B♭. 4. E♭ alto. 5. Double Bell (duplex) form adapted to B♭ bass or
baritone. The purpose of the smaller bell is to produce a contrasting tone somewhat of
trombone character, as against the broader tone usual to the instrument.

Sax evolved order out of this chaos, and the saxhorns above treated of contributed, in large measure, to that desirable end.

The playing compass of each member of the saxhorn family is given below. It is needless to remark that their musical possibilities are great, and all styles of articulation are quite as easy to perform as on any other brass instruments. Beyond this, the superior quality of tone should lead bandmasters to more general incorporation of the complete family in their organizations than at present obtains among them.

SAXHORNS, TREBLE-CLEF GROUP

SAXHORNS, BASS-CLEF GROUP

In this group all sounds are actual or concert pitch.

SCALE FOR FIVE-VALVE EUPHONIUM, OR B♭ BASS

NOTES PRODUCED WITH COMBINATION OF FOURTH VALVE ON THE E♭ BASS

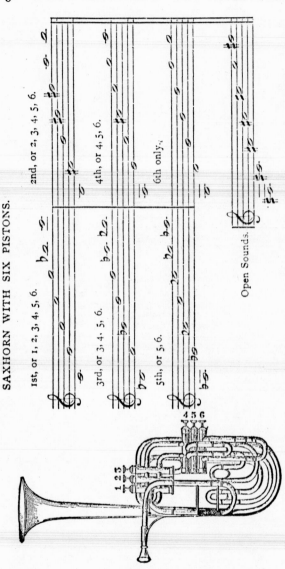

SAXHORN WITH SIX PISTONS.

This instrument was designed by Sax to overcome the discrepancies incidental to a three-piston instrument. As will be noticed, the open sounds are produced from the full length of tubing, and each other sequence has a piston for itself, thus conducing to accurate intonation.

CHAPTER X

INSTRUMENTS OF PERCUSSION

DRUMS. Kettledrums, or tympani, employed in the orchestra and cavalry band, and sometimes in the concert wind-band, have definable resonance, that is, by increasing or relaxing the tension, by use of screws set around their circumference, they may be tuned to each chromatic semitone within the scale of an octave. The drums are unequal in size, the larger one producing, by successive alterations, all sounds upwards within the interval of a fifth from its lowest tone, and the smaller one, similarly, carrying the scale to a sound an octave above the lowest one of the larger drum. Thus:

From which it will be apparent that they may be tuned at intervals of a minor or major third, perfect or imperfect fourth or fifth and so on. Generally speaking they are tuned to give the tonic and dominant of the composition in which they are introduced, in some instances from

dominant to tonic upwards, in others from tonic to
dominant downwards, thus: [music notation] .

The Javanese use an almost
complete scale of kettledrums, arranged in convenient
manner, which example furnishes a hint from Orient
to Occident of development that could not fail to be
effective in the modern orchestra. For, as our kettle-

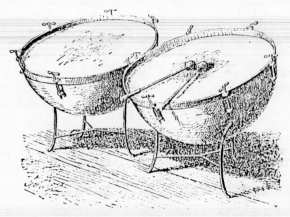

ORCHESTRAL KETTLEDRUMS.

drums are now made, they may be employed to reënforce
tonic and dominant (or occasionally other) harmonies
only, and thus be consonant, or, if elsewhere introduced,
become discordant elements in the orchestra. Berlioz
recommended employment of other drums, and to each
pair a drummer. The Javanese accomplish all he suggested with only one player.

Kettledrums are played with sticks having padded
heads, the "stick" being made from some flexible material

such as cane or whalebone. Single stroke, double stroke and rolls are played with ease, in any degree of force from extreme *pianissimo* to the most resounding *fortissimo;* consequently they are invaluable instruments in working up a *crescendo*, or *vice versa*.

CAVALRY DRUM.

All drums are described as having a stretched disk of elastic parchment to be struck with a stick. But kettledrums differ from other pulsatile instruments in having their single elastic disk stretched over large metal basins, which act as resonators. Hence their definable sounds.

THE SMALL DRUM, variously known as "side drum," from the manner in which it is carried, or "snare drum,"

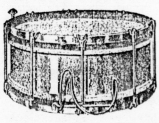

SIDE DRUM.

by reason of the several "snares" or gut strings stretched across its lower parchment disk. This drum is employed to reënforce rhythms in their various forms and aid the production of *crescendo* and *diminuendo*, which can be accomplished by certain "strokes" of its two sticks, known variously as "single" or "double

strokes," "flams," "paradiddles," "rolls" and so on.   To
the snare drummer is usually confided the use of certain
characteristic elements known as "traps," also the xylophone, bells, etc.

THE BASS DRUM is a three- or four-fold enlargement of
the former and like it has two parchment disks, or heads,

BASS DRUM.

strained to suitable ten-
sion by leathern tugs,
acting on rope attached
for the purpose to two
straining hoops, or by
screws set on their cir-
cumference, acting on
metal rods.   This latter
method is more generally
used in connection with
the snare drum than for
its larger colleague.   The
stick used, which must
be somewhat flexible, has
a padded head about
the size of a tennis ball.

CYMBALS, usually employed in pairs, are formed of
circular metal disks, varying in sizes, each one having at
its center a concavity, pierced in the middle for insertion
of a looped carrier or holder, made of leather through
which the player may pass his fingers to obtain his grip.

The best cymbals are the Chinese, or Turkish, so called. They are made of a composition of metals, similar to the substance in large bells, are quite thin, vibrate very freely and are turned or "flared" slightly outwards on their outer circumference.   For special gong-like effects one cymbal may be struck with a bass-drum stick, but, as a rule, they are clashed together, which should be effected

by an up or down slanting stroke, in order to obtain their vibrations in most free form. A direct or straight blow deadens their vibrations very much. "Their quivering or shrill sounds — the noise of which predominates over all other noises of the orchestra — ally themselves

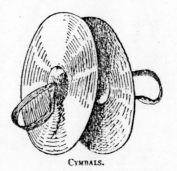

CYMBALS.

incomparably well, in certain cases, either with sentiments of extreme ferocity (then united to sharp whistlings of piccolo, flutes and to the strokes of the kettledrum, or small drum) or with the feverish excitement of a bacchanalian orgy, where revelry verges on frenzy." — *Berlioz.* The custom of attaching one cymbal to the bass drum is not commendable, however desirable it may be from an economical point of view.

THE GLOCKENSPIEL, formerly used more frequently than is now the case in marching bands, was formed of about an octave of flat metal bars, hung in a brass or white metal lyre-shaped frame, ornamented with colored horsehair tassels and set upon a turned wooden handle.

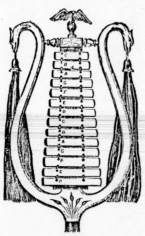

MILITARY BAND GLOCKENSPIEL.

The bars were tapped with a metal beater, or hammer affixed to a flexible handle, and the instrument was carried directly in front of the player, the lyre frame being about on a level with his head. The pitch was usually B♭ or A♭. This form seems to have succeeded one in which the bells were saucer-like in form, the same being mounted on a metal rod passing through holes in their center. Occasionally a regular small bell was pendent from each of the ornamental curves on the upper part of the lyre frame.

BELLS, so called, or *carillon*, are another form of the glockenspiel. They range in compass from one to two octaves (in C), with all chromatic semitones, and, in form of flat metal bars, are laid on lateral frames in a box, diatonic tones being on one, with chromatic notes on another, in suitable juxtaposition. The player having two strikers — flexible handles with small round metal heads — can attain great speed in execution. These contrivances may be had fitted with a keyboard similar with that of a piano, a method of construction which lends facility in performance.

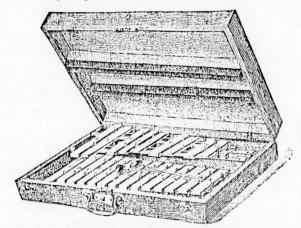

ORCHESTRA OR BAND BELLS, "CARILLON."

THE XYLOPHONE is similar in principle, but as the bars and strikers are made of wood, it emits a very different quality of tone, hollow but loud and somewhat "tubby" in character, but nevertheless effective. Descriptive

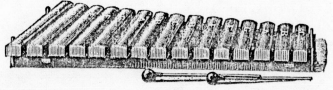

XYLOPHONE.

music offers a field for employment of all the foregoing instruments on the bell-like principle of vibration. It should be noted that double notes are not effective in performance, for reasons elsewhere given.

THE TRIANGLE, as the name implies, is a metal rod instrument bent to triangular form; the ends of the rod not

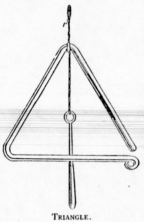

being united permits free vibration through its length. It is struck singly, or titillated, to produce a shivering effect, in the lower closed corner, by means of a short metal rod. To the upper corner, or apex of the triangle, a string loop is attached by which the player holds the instrument.

TRIANGLE.

TRAPS is the generic term for a multitude of contrivances designed for use in characteristic or descriptive music. Some have definite musical tones, others have not. Of the first class are instruments imitative of the calls of birds, as the cuckoo, quail, lark, etc.; of the second, much the more numerous, are the cock crow, baby cry, call of the katydid, engine whistle, sand paper on wooden slabs to imitate shuffling feet, clog

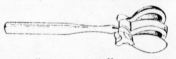

CASTAGNETS WITH HANDLE.

dance, castagnets, tambourine, tom-tom, sheet iron to imitate thunder, sleigh bells and so on without end. They all have their use, and, it may be said, abuse; and, while they may appeal to the ears of an uncultivated public, preferring *outre* effects to legitimate music, cannot fairly be accorded position as essentials in the instrumentation of a wind-band or other artistic organization.

Now, a few words on the history and universality of some of the foregoing instruments of percussion. The Egyptians used several kinds of drums, two of which were akin to our tambourines and another of triangular shape. They had long drums with two heads, a small conical hand drum and, also, a kettledrum very similar in form with that of the present day. The Hebrews, Grecians and Romans employed the same forms of drum in

TAMBOURINE.

social, religious and military functions. The Hebrew drum, *toph*, is said to have been a sort of small kettledrum. As the name *toph* is held by some to be generic

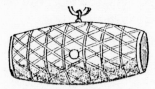

EGYPTIAN DRUM.

HEBREW DRUM, "TOPH."

rather than specific, doubt exists as to whether that name correctly designates that particular kettledrum — which illustrations show to resemble a rather shallow bowl with stretched skin head and double-knobbed drumstick, apparently to be gripped at its middle — or some other form.

Crusaders returning from Palestine are responsible for the appearance and use of drums in Western Europe.

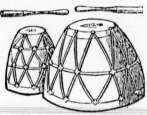

The practice of carrying drums suspended across the neck of a horse was copied from the Arabs, as also was the "snare" or side drum, and their introduction credited to the above source.

ANCIENT POLISH KETTLEDRUM.

Drums, in Chaucer's day, were termed *naker*, and drummers, *nakerers*. That term is derived from the Arabian word *nagarah*, which appears to have kinship with the East Indian *naguar*, a drum with one head. The name "knackers," applied to the old colored minstrel "bones," was, no doubt, derived from the above *naker*.

The aborigines of Africa evince great fondness for drums, of which they possess quite a variety. Some are made entirely of wood, others have one or two skin heads, according to tribe or usage. One of the most

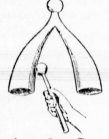

AFRICAN SIGNAL TUBE.

degenerate tribes of mankind, the South African Bosjesmen, use a rather unique drum, simply a wooden bowl, with tightly stretched skin head, into which they pour water to regulate the pitch. Double drums are used in the Congo regions, and among the negroes of northern Africa a cylinder, larger at one of its ends than at the other, is formed from the tamarind tree. The ends are covered with goat skin from which the hair has been removed. The heads are tightly strained and laced together with thongs, and their tension recovered or maintained by aid of heat from a fire. In parts of Western Africa it is customary to affix human skulls to drums by way of decoration. (?) Drums are employed throughout the continent to warn off unwelcome nocturnal visitors, for communication among the separated kraals of a tribe, to sound alarms, drown the

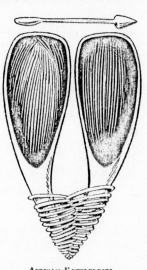

AFRICAN KETTLEDRUM.

ARUWIMI WAR DRUM AND WOMAN.

cries of victims of war, stimulate revelry, celebrate a victory, at religious rites and to solemnize a funeral. In some tribes all the drummers assemble to beat up the new moon, beginning *largo, pianissimo*, when first it appears, and continuing to increase in speed and force of drumming as the luminary ascends to midheaven. Women have the prescriptive right among the Aruwimi to sound the alarm for war on a very large drum kept for that particular purpose. It is a wide stretch from Wahuma to the Sandwich Islands,

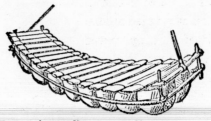

AFRICAN XYLOPHONE OR MARIMBA.

yet in the matter of drums they are by no means remote. Each possesses at least one drum nearly identical in form.

Instruments corresponding with the xylophone are found in two styles in Africa and Burmah, termed in the former *marimba*, in the latter *patolah*.

The Chinese have eight kinds of drum, named, *tsou-kou, yukow, hinen-kou, kin-kou, tao-kou, ya-kou, po-fou* and *po-sou*. The *hinen-kou* is a drum of immense proportions, raised on a pedestal several feet high. The tones of the *po-fou* are modified by partially filling its body with rice husks. That people celebrate the advent of the New Year by incessant drumming throughout night and day. Their martial neighbors, the Japanese, have many and similar drums. One, of indigenous origin, *Taiko*, resembles an hourglass in form and can be played at both ends. They have also a side drum, which they call *kakko*.

Metal drums, and others of usual materials, are used in Java. But the Javanese use a kettledrum combination, worthy of description, unique of structure and in manner of playing thereon. Its name is *tseing*, *S'hing* or *Boundaw*.

It consists of "a collection of small drums suspended around the inside of a richly carved frame of wood about three feet high. They regularly diminish in size from that of a two-gallon measure to that of a pint. The player sits within the circle and with his hands

BOUNDAW, JAVA KETTLEDRUMS, AND PLAYER.

produces a rude tone or accompaniment. Drumsticks are not often used. In the full band the Boundaw is never omitted." The illustration shows twelve drums included in the Boundaw, which might be made to include each note save one of our chromatic scale.

In Lapland, drums in some form are as general and considered as essential in the home as is the piano with us. The Lapland drum is thought to possess talismanic, prophetic and psychic powers, as well as the usual but more prosaic attributes.

According to Oviedo, the Cuban Indians prepared and used human skins for the heads of their drums. Bernard Diaz designates as a "hellish instrument" a certain drum he saw in a Mexican temple, the heads of which were made from the skins of great serpents. Whatever impression that drum may have made on him, more recent writers describe Mexican drums in somewhat less harsh terms. The *teponaztli* is cylindrical in shape and made entirely of wood, and the *huehuetl*, "curiously carved and painted and covered at the top with carefully prepared deer skin," was similar in form but larger, being about three feet long. The latter was beaten by the hands, the former with sticks, the knobs of which were formed of an elastic gum called *ule*. These drums were common in the days of Cortes, and are said to be still used in remote parts of the country by descendants of the Aztecs.

The foregoing shows the ancient lineage of the drum and its universality in past and present days. Drum-beats girdle the globe and their vibrations are among those touches of nature that "make all the world kin."

CHAPTER XI

THE BANDMASTER

THE term "bandmaster" is taken to signify master of the wind-band. Mastery implies possession of power; in this case, special knowledge and certain fitness, which may be assisted in development by education but can only exist in perfection as an inherent trait of artistic character or temperament. Lacking this high essential, it matters not how profound a bandmaster's learning may be, how painstaking his teaching, how exacting his methods in the rehearsal room, their ultimate result, as shown by performance of his band, will be unsatisfactory. Precision of attack, correctness of dynamic expression, accuracy of tone, tune and time may all be present, but failing the infusion of emotional expression, the vital spark which vivifies and illuminates the inner meaning of musical works, or, if there be wanting, the contagious enthusiasm that shall arouse in each member of the organization high impulses commensurate with his own, the playing of his band, while pedagogically perfect, will inspire the feeling of being learnedly dull. Bandmasters, like poets, are born, not made. This verity must not be taken to imply that education is unnecessary. On the contrary, it is often necessary to awaken the latent talent, or genius, and always requisite as a guide to direction and attainment of its fullest manifestation.

The foregoing statement, as well as those which follow, are necessary to counteract the prevailing opinion that any instrumentalist is qualified to fill the position of bandmaster. Specialists are they who confine themselves to the cultivation of some one branch in particular of their profession. A soloist, or ordinary band or orchestra instrumentalist, is usually a specialist in that sense. He confines his energies, more or less, to the arduous task of mastering the technical difficulties of some instrument in particular, and frequently — too much — neglects to inform himself of other matters considered essential to the acquirement of a sound musical education. An instrumentalist in ordinary thus becomes fitted as one of the parts of a machine, truly essential in his place, but not qualified by limitations of education to exercise the functions of a controlling power. A sailor before the mast, or a soldier in the ranks, may be most efficient as sailor or soldier, but no one, on general principles, would admit either as being fitted to take command of a ship or a regiment. Yet this unsound position is recognized as justifiable in its application to the appointment of bandmasters generally in the United States, and particularly in government (army and navy) wind-bands, by which the mode of procedure begets official sanction.

Abroad, where bandmasters and bandsmen are paid much less than they are here for their services, bandmasters can only attain to such rank as the result of successfully passing a very severe musical examination. This method obtains in France, Belgium, Italy and other countries, and from it results the recognition of bandmasters as musicians of high attainments, worthy of professional confidence and respect. In England, in order to do away with conditions similar to those in the United States, a Royal Military School of Music was established about sixty years ago, at Kneller Hall, near London, for the purpose of training bandmasters and soloists for the army. (A similar institution was later founded for the navy.) British army bandmasters must graduate from that school. The course is three years and the curriculum severe. Admission is confined to musicians serving in the army, who are required to pass an entrance examination. The result of the foregoing methods of careful selection of chiefs is apparent in the playing of bands under their direction and excellence obtaining among individual members of the same. Bands, such as those of the Garde Républicaine of Paris, the Guides of Brussels, the Guards of London, supply wind instrumentalists to opera and symphony orchestras of their respective cities. It is a matter for regret that conditions, similar to the foregoing, do not obtain in this country.

As must be apparent from the above considerations, the essential qualifications of a bandmaster are, to say the least, varied and broad in scope. Tersely stated they should include:

(1) Skill on some wind instrument in particular.

(2) Practical knowledge of all other wind instruments, that is, to be able to play them more or less well.

(3) Knowledge of the theory and practice of music, including harmony,

counterpoint, composition, instrumentation, forms, and acquaintance with acoustics in relation to wind instruments, as well as musical history in general and in particular.

(4) Capacity to read "scores" and interpret them.

(5) Pedagogic ability; teaching, tuning and toning of the wind-band and

(6) Capacity for direction, otherwise conducting.

Just as water, under ordinary circumstances, will not rise higher than its level, so may we never expect to find a wind-band better than its director. If he be a man of high attainments, ideals and energy, he will lift the quality of the organization towards his level; but should he be the reverse, the band will sink to his status. Operation of the law of cause and effect being inevitable, it is futile to expect good bands as the result of employment of incompetent bandmasters.

Hence, it is obvious and requisite that the bandmaster should be a man of good musical and other education, instinctively refined, of magnetic temperament, and of gentlemanly deportment. Possessed of those qualifications he will command the esteem, confidence and respect of the musical profession and the general public.

CHAPTER XII

SOME FALLACIES AS TO WIND INSTRUMENTS

It is impossible to state where the idea originated that over-blowing permanently injures the intonation of a wind instrument. So obvious, indeed, is this fallacy, that it appears almost a waste of time to refer to it. Yet, illogical as it may appear, that idea is still current, as well among amateurs as among some professionals, who should know better. Truly, he who could produce such a result would have been hailed victor in musical contests connected with the Pythian games. It is feared that he would have required some contrivance stronger than the *phorbeion* to bandage and sustain his facial muscles.

Sound is the result of a vibratory condition of the atmosphere. Musical instruments are means by which the air may be set in motion with speed and periodicity, sufficiently rapid and uniform to be appreciable to our ears as concordant sounds. In any case, aerial vibrations themselves, acting upon the delicate machinery of our ears, are the sole cause of sound, and the explanation as to their effect. This fact upsets the theory, advanced by certain makers and agents, that vibrations of the body of an instrument are contributory to sound production.

It is said, the human ear is capable of distinguishing sounds beyond the limits of vibrations necessary to produce the lowest tone of a string bass, or the highest sound of a piccolo, the range of which extends from 42 to 4800 vibrations per second.   In fact, we know it is possible to hear the tones of a 32-foot organ pipe imparting 16 vibrations a second, and we are conscious from experience with certain other mediums that the ear can recognize sound at greater altitude than the highest tone of the piccolo. Vibrations are of two forms, — *longitudinal*, as is the case with the air column of wind instruments, and *transverse*, as those resulting from bowing, plucking or striking a stretched string. The length of the air column formed within a tube affects the pitch of a wind instrument, and its width — that is diameter — is responsible for breadth of tone.   Narrow tubes give incisive high tones, wide tubes produce broad ones, but the differences of pitch subsisting between soprano, alto, tenor or bass instruments is entirely dependent upon length of tube. Breadth of tone, generally speaking, is coincident with diameter, and pitch with length of tubes, and is in no way the result of any molecular disturbance, if such exist, of material employed to confine and mold the air column on its passage outwards.   The formative medium employed at the moment of inception, as the lips of player on instruments with cupped mouthpieces, and flutes, reeds of the clarionet, or oboe, affect quality or color of tone; as well also, but in less degree, does form of tube, whether conical or cylindrical, broad or narrow, as above stated.

Longitudinal vibrations of an air column divide themselves into segments, in which they expand and contract, and nodes, or points of rest. The following illustrations show the frequency and occurrence of segments and nodes of an open pipe when the air column is producing sounds in the ratio of 1, 2, 3:

Fundamental Tone

Node

Segment   Segment

1st Harmonic
or Overtone   S   N   S   N   S

2nd Harmonic
or Overtone   S   N   S   N   S   N   S

Segments and nodes go on increasing in frequency until the upper limit of the harmonic series is reached. The foregoing will help to explain why dents or punctures of brass tubes occurring at nodal points may have little effect, also why they seriously and injuriously affect their tone and tune if on the segments.

Mr. J. D. Blaikley of London illustrated this peculiarity in a lecture delivered before the students at the Royal Military School of Music some time ago. For the purpose he had a bugle constructed, divided into segments, according to the occurrence of the nodes, which he could unite or disunite at will. The tube was so arranged as to admit the insertion of thin metal disks having a few small perforations to permit passage of the breath. Those disks were intended to prevent oscillations of the air across the nodal positions, thus demonstrating their nonexistence. Placing three disks within the bugle and then blowing into it, he showed conclusively that they offered no impediment to the production of the note C, but that they did prevent the production of any other notes possible to the bugle under ordinary conditions. While it was apparent that insertion of disks at nodal points do not influence the pitch of the tube note, he made it evident that small modifications in the form of any one of the sections of a tube will affect it most seriously. He demonstrated this by replacing two portions of the tube where segments occur with others of slightly differing taper. In the experiment he endeavored to produce an octave, but fell short, in so doing, by about one semitone, a fact from which the precept may be deduced that prompt remedial attention to bruises or leakages is essential to tone, tune and an instrument's well-being in general.

Another fallacy prevalent among instrumentalists is, that tone color is influenced by, and in fact is more or less dependent on the character of the material used in building a wind instrument. They point to the violin and the piano and say, "If material there assists vibration, why may it not do so in case of wind instruments?" The answer is immediately available. There can be no analogy between the two classes of instruments in direc-

tion of the query, because the violin body acts as a resonator, or amplifier of sound, and the piano is equipped
with a sounding board, otherwise reflector and amplifier;
whereas the tube of a wind instrument is simply a sound
conveyor, and in no sense can it, by sympathetic oscillations, enhance volume or character of tone by reflecting
or amplifying its requisite vibrations.   Hardness of material and internal finish of the interior of a tube are the
only conditions required as supplementary to length and
width for production of sound.   Brass is employed, not
because it is thick or thin, or that it vibrates any more
freely than other metals, but for the simple reason that it
is easily bent, or curved into any form required in the
construction of wind instruments.   Experiments with
paper, plaster of Paris, wood, gutta-percha, horn and
other materials have been made, and in each case it has
been shown that the substance used had no effect on tone
color, providing only that acoustic requirements were
fulfilled.

Again, there are players who hold the opinion that he
who can inject wind into a tube with greater force than
some colleague will produce the best tone.   When it is
understood that breath travels through an instrument at
a rate of from three to nine inches the second, relatively
with size of instrument, it will be perceived that the
speed of inrush of breath is not a very important factor.
To demonstrate this, have a couple of small holes bored
immediately under the rim of a cup mouthpiece; then
below those holes stretch a piece of goldbeater's skin, or

similar material, entirely across the mouthpiece, so as to prevent the breath from passing into the instrument, thus compelling it to seek egress through the two holes above referred to. It will be found that the breath striking against the stretched skin will throw the air column within the instrument into vibration, and as a result all sounds peculiar to it can be obtained in their proper intervals and quality, the only element lacking being that of intensity, otherwise force. This proves that vibration of the air column acts independently of immediate contact with the player's breath, and eliminates the theory of possession of Herculean wind power as a prerequisite of good tone, for, as has been shown, that quality is present even when that force is much curtailed.

Still another fallacy is one connected with the subject of temperature and its influence on the pitch of instruments. As every musician knows, cold and heat affect pitch, in the one case by lowering, in the other by elevating; but the fallacy lies, in this instance, in the failure to attribute that rise or fall somewhat to atmospheric conditions and only in part to the temperature of the instrument itself. Mr. Blaikley, already mentioned, made some experiments going to show that some of the phenomena of rise and fall of pitch must be sought elsewhere than in the conditional temperature of the body of an instrument alone. He remarks: "The true cause of sharpening is the effect of heat upon the air, which is so great as to cause a rise of pitch of a semitone between $37\frac{1}{2}°$

and 90° F., or say a quarter-tone between 47° and 73°, a very moderate range of temperature between winter and [an English] summer. This maximum range of vibration is modified in practice by the heat of the breath, which has more effect, proportionally, in cold weather than in hot, and therefore the difference between summer and winter pitch of instruments, when warmed with playing, is always less than would be due to extremes of temperature of the external air." Naturally temperature of the tube itself modifies intonation, but, as must be apparent, rise of pitch among wind instruments in a concert room, for instance, is influenced to some extent by the rise of temperature natural to a closed room, wherein conditions of heat are accelerated and increased by addition of animal caloric.

The foregoing present a few fallacies prevalent among musicians, which seem to have had their origin in observation of effects only, and want of consideration of their underlying causes, and thereafter announcing as facts for belief that which investigation shows to be, at best, but hasty conclusions.

CHAPTER XIII

TONE COLOR AND TONE BUILDING

TONE color is one of the most beautiful incidents of musical sound. In France the word *timbre* is applied to it; in Germany, *klangfarbe;* while in England, investigators have sought to render it intelligible by combining the words "clang" and "tint," thus forming the compound *clangtint*. Tone color, timbre, klangfarbe and clangtint mean the same thing, and are terms used to designate differing shades of tone, resulting from sounds identical in pitch and intensity but varying by method of production and medium from whence they proceed.

The sensation we know as musical sound is the result of aerial vibrations communicated to the ear by sound waves of regular and periodic flow. Immediate intensity impresses itself on the ear by sounds at higher or lower pitch, which, fitting into our scale, are designated accordingly. These sounds are not, as is thought by the uninitiated, simple, but on the contrary formed, and in measure characterized, by a combination of others, much more feeble, arising from the division of a pipe or string into segments, and accompanying the prime or fundamental tone, when a string or the air column within a pipe is thrown into vibration. The accompanying feeble sounds are termed "harmonics," and their fusion with the fundamental produces tones more or less agreeable proportionally with the balance obtaining among them. Constituent vibrations of musical sound can be optically demonstrated by means of resonators, Chladni's plates, or an instrument invented by König, by which it becomes possible to render those component vibrations visible to a large audience. König's contrivance is thus described in Blaserna's "Theory of Sound": "The apparatus is composed of eight resonators adapted to the harmonic series of the fundamental note c. At the back of each one an India-rubber tube puts the orifice in communication with a capsule, closed by an elastic membrane. In front of this gas enters and burns under the form of a small, very mobile flame. Eight flames, therefore, correspond to the eight resonators. When the air vibrates in one of the resonators the vibration is communicated to the flame, and its vibrations are observed by means of a revolving mirror, which is turned by a handle. In order to know if the sound of a given instrument or of the human voice contains harmonics, and what they may be, all that is needful is to produce close to the apparatus a note corresponding in pitch to the large resonator — that is to say c — which represents the fundamental note. Then, if there be harmonics, they will set the resonators in action, and thence the corresponding flames, and a glance at the revolving mirror is all that is required in order to recognize them immediately." The ordinary phonograph affords an illustration of how vibrations may be made visible, and, furthermore, demonstrates reflection of musical sounds.

Brass instruments with cupped mouthpiece, having pistons or slides designed to elongate the main tube by seven successive additions, can be caused to produce seven series of harmonics, each a semitone lower than the other. Flutes, oboes, bassoons, saxophones and sarrusophones have harmonics identical in sequence with those of the open pipe, as also have string instruments and the human voice. Clarionets differ; their harmonics, being those of a stopped pipe, are in the ratio of 1, 3, 5, 7.

Tone color is largely influenced by number and quality of harmonics. The human voice, being richest in them, is the most musical of all sound-producing organisms, and string instruments rank next in order. Instruments poor in harmonics are weak and thin of tone. For instance, the tone of a tuning fork, which has none, is extremely feeble, and to become distinct, at even a short distance away, needs to be reënforced by contact with some body acting as a resonator, or amplifier. When the lower harmonics prevail, the tone is of broad, open, soft character, of course subject to modifications contingent on size of the instrument; but if the upper harmonics be strong, as in the trumpet and trombone, the tone is shrill, penetrating and vibrant to a degree. Thus, it will be seen, diversity of tone color observable among instruments is connected with the phenomenon of musical tones.

Again, tone color differentiates as do the methods by

which sound is produced. Impact, as in the pianoforte, friction, as of the bow on a violin string, vibration of reeds and rush of wind against the sharp edge of the mouth hole of a flute, are among the causal noises entering into and helping to impart individuality to tone color. The manner in which a bow is drawn or pushed across the strings of a violin, according to position, being forceful or relatively weak, modifies quality of tone color. Something similar may be said of the embouchure in case of wind instruments, as also of the method of striking the keys of a pianoforte, where it may be caused to vary from the refined quality of a Paderewski to the coarse emanations of a piano pounder of the dance hall. Irregular bowing, faulty methods and overblowing wind instruments, and so on, by disturbing the balance that should subsist between harmonics and their fundamental, deleteriously affect tone color. This fact points to the conclusion that careful methods of sound production are requisite among instrumentalists and vocalists.

W. H. Stone in his work "On Sound," treating of tonal characteristics of wind instruments, gives the result of some interesting experiments made to determine the average wind pressure necessary to produce notes on certain instruments. Grouping them in three classes, as flutes, reeds and instruments with cupped mouthpieces, he points out that all of them require two essential organs operative for production of sound, viz.: the wind chest, which in this case is the human thorax (chest, etc.), and the embouchure, that is, lips, contributary

muscles and that part of an instrument through which
the wind enters. The method by which he determined
the pressures within the thorax is thus described: "A
water gauge was connected with a small curved piece of
tube by means of a long flexible rubber pipe. The curved
tube being inserted in the angle of the mouth, did not,
after a little practice, interfere with the ordinary playing
of the instrument. The various notes were then sounded
successively, and the height at which the column stood
was noted. The following table of pressures was obtained as an average of many experiments:

TABLE OF PRESSURES

Oboe	9 to 17 ins.	Cornet	10 to 34 ins.
Clarionet	15 to 18 ins.	Trumpet	12 to 33 ins.
Bassoon	12 to 24 ins.	Euphonium	3 to 40 ins.
Horn	5 to 27 ins.	Bombardon	3 to 36 ins.

The table is interesting as exhibiting the relative
average wind pressure necessary on the several instruments to produce tones of good quality at medium
intensity.

A somewhat similar experiment was conducted by
J. J. Chediwa of Odessa at L'Exposition Universelle,
Paris, 1889. He termed the instrument by which he
established pressures, *dynamometre musicale*. It regis-
tered dynamic pressure of the air column of brass instruments as it left the tube and came in contact with the
atmosphere, showing degree of pressure involved when
producing various notes in differing degrees of force.

The foregoing contrivances are among the paraphernalia by which it becomes possible to discern, at least, the operation of the laws of sound in their vibratory motions, already palpable by the eardrums, and remove theories from the field of speculation .into the region of demonstrable facts. Consideration of them teaches necessity for study of tone color, from the moment when instruction begins until, having garnered knowledge by the way, the student may say "I have conquered." The coarse tones of a young beginner or a careless musician present a vivid contrast with those of the finished player, wherein are found mobility, richness, warmth, resonancy and all qualities conducive to perfect homogeneity and a high state of development of tone color.

Conformation of the mouth exercises an important bearing on tone color, for, as is well known, harmonics vary according to the position assumed by the interior of the mouth, lips and teeth when singing the vowels A, E, O, U and I, changing the tone color of the same note as the singer passes from one to the other. The experience of wind instrumentalists point in the same direction, as changes in mouth and lips incidental to varying range of compass must exert their influence on tone color. Furthermore, conformation of mouth peculiar to each individual player will to some extent modify tone color, which explains, at least in part, the many shades or diversities observable among players, even when using instruments identical in construction and from the same maker. Impetus of the air column originates in the

thorax, and is somewhat modified by the position of the
larynx, tongue and mouth in general. · Each part must
exercise its function in orderly succession or simultane-
ously, controlled by the player, and thus, in origination,
form, direction and power create the force that is to set
the air column in vibration. Failure to employ those
contributory agencies with wisdom and discretion involves the penalty of imperfect tone color, which in its
perfection, with the impinging requirements of correct
tune, are two of the most essential qualities demanded in
wind-instrument playing, to be recognized as agreeable
to and acceptable by cultured musicians.

Corelated with tone color is what may be termed
tone building, that is, the constructive process which,
by hewing and polishing each individual tone in the compass of his instrument, a musician creates an edifice of
sound which, similarly with the perfect realization of an
architect, shall present an harmonious assemblage of
components uniting to form a building of graceful proportions, thus exhibiting, at one and the same time, the
effects of patient industry and observance of the laws
of art.

Musicians of experience are cognizant of the immense
labor required in the process of building up a good tone.
The voice requires much polishing to become a medium
of correct musical expression. Manufactured wind instruments are simply implements for the production of
sound, and, no matter how carefully made, do not absolve
the player from the necessity for unremitting labor in

upbuilding of tone, true in acoustic quality and character of his particular instrument, but tinged by his taste, temperament, or, in a word, individuality.

That diversity in shades of tone exists among voices and instruments of the same kinds is a recognized fact. Conformity to some supposed standard — as established by reference to a remarkable singer or player — is neither possible nor desirable, for those divergencies, when united in chorus, orchestra or wind-band, produce a composite tone, preferable in richness of texture to the unisonal effect of a number of voices or instruments emitting individual tones absolutely identical in color. To say, then, that variety of shade in tone color exhibits lack of cultivation because it does not conform in requirements with some preconceived standard is incorrect, as much so as to say that roses lack in loveliness because of their want of uniformity. Differentiation being admitted, it follows that characteristic quality of class, modified as it will be by personal idiosyncrasy, should be developed to the limits of good taste.

Fusion of the various shades of tone color in the wind-band goes to make up a composite whole, but in order that this composite tone shall be perfect, it is requisite that each of its constituent elements shall be equally so, taking into account, of course, the personal equation controlled by good taste. For instance, assuming an unisonal sound as the joint emanation from all instruments of the wind-band, it will be obvious that its quality is conditional for excellence upon perfect balance, unanimity of tune, and agreeable tone color among the elements of the organism.

Whether or not we regard voices or instruments as mediums of musical utterance, influence of the temperament of a player must be recognized in the single instrument and in the collective effort of any body of musicians. Otherwise it would be impossible to account for those variations of tone shades which charm us equally as individual shades or as distinctive tone colors of a class. A rose emits an odor differing from that of a lily and a lily from that of a violet, and all three are dissimilar in appearance. Yet to pronounce one less fragrant or beautiful than the others would create a distinction calling forth dissent. As a truth, among things inherently beautiful it is impossible to create strong distinctions. Contrasts of form, color and odor are apparent, but beauty is constant and eternal. We may say this thing pleases us, or that one is distasteful, for there we express personal opinion only; but if, on the other hand, we dogmatically insist that the thing pleasing us is alone excellent, we are wrong, and by so insisting become unreasonable, arrogating to ourselves a right inherent in no man. The analogy holds in the world of tones, where that which appeals to us and influences the statement of our preference has not always a similar effect on our neighbor. Want of recognition of this truth has led to bitter disagreements in the art world in the past and still continues to provide material for critics to wrangle over and friends to discuss with more or less warmth. There is one point upon which all may agree, — blight on the petals of flowers mar their beauty, and defective, blighted intonation among instruments equally injures tone. Furthermore, if the notes of the scale differ in intensity, clearness of expression, or if certain defects inherent in voices or instruments be not eliminated, and the whole thus brought up to a general level of excellence, the tone builder has failed and the result cannot be good.

Tone building, like building of more material objects, is a cumulative process. Beginning with the first effort to produce musical sounds from an instrument, to the moment when it can be said that mastery of those sounds has been attained, in all their requirements and possibilities of absolute accuracy of tune, interminable degrees of dynamic force and the quality of living expression, the accretion is so slow as to become monotonous and tiresome. There are moments in the life of every man of artistic temperament when he despairs of attaining the goal of perfection. Nevertheless he persists, and by exercise of will power finally reaches the point where men praise his work, and his labors as a tone builder become, in some measure, satisfying to himself.

Two other essentials associated with the consideration of tone color and tone building are " pitch " and "amplitude."

Pitch, in its limited application, refers to the position any given note maintains in relation to an assumed standard, but in a broader sense is understood to include "tune" or "intonation."

As one of the properties of musical sounds, apparent to every one, pitch is the result of atmospheric vibrations communicated to the ear in intermittent, periodic shocks of greater or less rapidity. When the impinging aerial vibrations are slow, pitch of the resultant sound is low; when very rapid, it is high. Periodicity of vibrations is essential; otherwise, instead of music, noise would result. From the fact that rapidity of vibration determines the pitch of musical sounds, it follows that each is dependent for position in the scale on some given number of such vibrations, just as much so as that a pound of sugar shall contain so many ounces or a yard of cloth so many inches. It is known that sounds inaudible to man are heard by the lower order of animals and that among men there exist many differences in aural sensitiveness. In general, the range of human hearing extends over something like eleven octaves, ranging from 16 to 4800 vibrations a second.

There are several methods by which rapidity of vibrations may be determined, among them Savart's ratchet wheel, an instrument termed "Siren," and deductions by mathematics, when length, weight and tension of a string is known, or length and diameter of a tube has been established. Vibrations are said to be double, that is the motion of the air wave consists of a to-and-fro oscillation somewhat like the pendulum of a clock. The sound C with its fundamental stated at 16 vibrations, doubling at the rise of each octave, as 16, 32, 64, 128, 256, 512, and so on, represented by pipes, the frequency of their vibrations being in inverse ratio with the length, as 32, 16, 8, 4 or 2 feet, etc., lies at the root of the whole subject of pitch. The product of 512 vibrations is expressed by at what is known as *philosophical pitch*. There exists some disagreement in practice, and the note above shown varies from 512 to 517, which is the low pitch established by French law, and 540 vibrations the second, as in high pitch.

Since musical sounds are resultants of quantitative atmospheric vibrations, it must be obvious that exact proportionate ratio must obtain between all notes of the scale; this requirement is just as absolute as that each inch in a yardstick shall have an equal number of fractional subdivisions. But, from certain contingent causes, possible variations in pitch, within the limits of even one octave, are practically limitless, for while there are only thirteen sounds, including first and last, admissible in the octave, each one is susceptible of more or less minute differentiations, resulting from mode of attack or production. Of the influence exerted by slight deviation from true pitch, pianoforte tuning affords an illustration, for there, in order to meet the requirements of the scale of equal temperament, the tuner must make his fifths about *one fiftieth of a semitone* too flat; otherwise the instrument would appear abominably out of tune. It has been estimated that ordinary ears can distinguish from fifty to a hundred sounds within the limits of an octave. Such being the case, there exists wide scope for deviations from accurate pitch which, if permitted in practice, must be more or less detrimental to homogeneity in individual playing and in collective performance, as in the wind-band.

Systematic, extremely critical education of the ear is the only safeguard against faulty intonation. The task is arduous, but the habit of playing in tune is an accomplishment which, once acquired, becomes a valuable possession more than compensatory of the labor involved. Incidentally, it may be suggested, a course of *solfeggio* will be found of great service in educating the ear. It teaches the mind to measure intervals and trains the ear to verify them in practice, better, perhaps, than any other method of instruction. To aim at rapidity of execution — a fault only too common — before the musical ear has been formed, works great injury; for hearing is blunted to such an extent that it afterwards becomes impossible to whet it and to acquire that sharp edge of tonal discernment so necessary to precision and accuracy of intonation.

As to volume, or, technically expressed, *amplitude* of sound, gradations are limited only by the capacity of the sound-producing medium, as may be perceived by comparing the voices of children and men or tones of flutes and tubas. Sounds are classed, in relation to strength, as loud and soft. A vigorous attack of the bow on a violin string will excite more atmospheric commotion than arises from a more gentle impact. Degrees of amplitude vary, but, no matter how powerful or weak sounds may be, the vibration quantity remains the same, provided always that accessories to production operate correctly and

uniformly at all times; thus, faulty method of attack, or of
conditions of embouchure, while not affecting proportional
strength of sounds, will materially influence their intonation, a fact showing the necessity for care in the exercise
of musical dynamics.

Sound may be sustained at any degree of force between loud and soft, or made to pass through many
gradations of intensity from *pianissimo* to *fortissimo*.
To establish an absolute standard of tonal dynamics
is impossible, but, assuming the player to have an
approximate idea of the capacity of his instrument, in
either direction he may formulate a guide for himself.
Musical nomenclature states seven degrees of force, thus:
ppp, pp, p, mf, f, ff and *fff*, the relative strength of which
must necessarily differ among individual players and
combinations of instruments.   A good working plan suggesting the mental effect of relative dynamics, as well as
evenness of force in duration, is to state the degrees by
lines, thus:

1	2	3	4	5	6	7
ppp	*pp*	*p*	*mf*	*f*	*ff*	*fff*

The use of such lines tends to impress the mind with
the necessity for sustaining tones evenly at the seven
degrees of strength, a requisite needing sedulous cultivation.   Next to these, augmentations and diminutions of
force, short or long continued, must be carefully prac-
ticed.   The symbols expressive of those qualities are

most appropriate; in fact none better could be conceived,
thus: Augmentation.　　Diminution.

Following the above come "explosive tones," so called,
symbolized variously by ⁀, ∧, *sf*, *sfz* and so on.

Control of relative dynamic expression is indispensable
to the process of tone building, for only by it can the
habit be acquired of giving to each tone its compara-
tive strength value, compatible with capacity of player
and instrument and the requirements of a composition.
Essential as is this requirement to the individual, it is
much more so in collective performance, for there dynamic
values must be so attempered and balanced that the tone
produced by any single instrument, or group of instruments — excepting where special effects be required —
shall not exceed that of another. Concerted playing
exhibits the nearest possible approach to an absolute
dynamic standard that can be advanced, and which
appears to lie about midway between *pianissimo* of the
feeblest instrument and *fortissimo* of the loudest.

From the foregoing observations it will be apparent
that tone color and tone building, as applied to wind
instruments, are not fanciful considerations, requirements
or theories, but on the contrary are essentials of tonal excellence, which must be thoroughly studied, their inter-
relations understood, and the benefit their development
will bring fully appreciated.

CHAPTER XIV

MUSICAL DYNAMICS

MUSIC is considered an emotional art. It appeals to the inner nature of man, by and through combinations of tones, or sequence of single notes in varying degrees of duration or elevation, rhythmic forms in frank or subtle alternations, changing modulations, and lastly by the quality of increasing or decreasing intensity of sound, which, under caption of Musical Dynamics, are now under consideration.

Composers, since the days of Bach, have always sought to express their ideas concerning the amount of dynamic force to be employed, in delivery of the various sections, motives, passages and so on, forming the body material of their works, by use of certain conventional signs, words and phrases. These indications are necessarily only relative in application, varying as to individual conception and limitations of the capacity of voices or instruments. The duty of a player is to follow them with care, and to endeavor, so far as in him lies, to fulfill the wishes of the composer and thus faithfully strive to utilize one of the many means at his disposal to develop and portray the true character of the work he is rendering. It is a matter for frequent complaint that musicians in wind-bands and orchestras are not so careful or faithful in this respect as in duty bound they ought to be. In his book "On Conducting," Richard Wagner found fault with the skilled instrumentalists of Germany for disregard of the requirements of dynamic signs and expression. Said he, "Let any conductor ask any orchestral instrument, no matter which, for a full prolonged *forte*, and he will find the player puzzled and will be astonished at the trouble to get what he asks for." Later on he remarks, "Now the strings produce the latter [*piano*] with ease, but the wind instruments, particularly the wood winds, do not." And again he says, "Of course it is easy enough to produce a buzzing vibration by gently passing the bow over the strings; but it requires great artistic command of the breath to produce a delicate pure tone upon a wind instrument." These strictures were not passed upon second- or third-rate players of an unmusical nation, but addressed to the best products of one reputed musical to its core. If then superior musicians were found lacking in appreciation and expression of simple dynamic elements by a master of the art, is it not fair to assume that they were equally, possibly more, disregardful of the variety of *nuance* not indicated by conventional words, letters or signs, and which are only inferable from the structural elements of a composition? The faults condemned by Wagner are world-wide and limited to no nation or class of musicians, excepting, of course, the cultured and conscientious. The latter recognize the importance attaching to the study of intensity of sound, as indicated by the usual formulæ, and understand also that while the former is of the body, so to say, equal if not greater value adheres to, and much more industry and intelligence is required for expression of intensity under the surface, not written, and which is of the spirit. This quality is vague, unmeaning to the average musician, or only dimly guessed at by him, though he may have spent many years in the profession.

The following table of letters, words and signs indicating varying degrees of tonal intensity comprises those most commonly employed:

DYNAMIC VOCABULARY

LETTERS, TERMS AND SIGNS OF EMPHASIS

TERM	PRONUNCIATION	MEANING
Pianissimo, *pp* or *ppp* .	*Peeah-nis'see-mo*	Very softly
Piano Assai, *pp* or *ppp*	*Peean'no as-sah'ee*	Very softly
Piano, *p*	*Peeah'no*	Softly
Meno piano, *mp*	*May'no Peeah'no*	{ Less soft than preceding *piano*
Più Piano	*P'yoo peeah'no*	Softer
Mezzo forte, *mf*	*Med'zo forr'tay*	Rather loud
Meno forte, *mf*	*May'no forr'tay*	{ Less loud than preceding *forte*
Poco forte, *pf*	*Po'ko forr'tay*	Rather loud
Forte, *f*	*Forr'tay*	Loud
Fortissimo, *ff* or *fff* ..	*For-tis'see-mo*	Loud as possible
Più Forte, *pf*	*P'yoo forr'tay*	Louder
Poco più forte	*Po'ko p'yoo forr'tay*	A little louder
Crescendo, *cres*	*Cray-shen'doh*	{ Gradually increasing loudness
Poco a poco crescendo.	*Po'ko a po'ko cray-shen'doh*	
Decrescendo	*Dee-cray-shen'doh*	{ Gradual diminution of sound
Diminuendo, *dim*	*Dee-mee-nooen'doh*	
Perdendosi	*Pair-den-do'see*	Dying away
Mancando	*Mahn-kahn'doh*	Subsiding
Smorendo	*Zmo-ren'doh*	Extinguishing
Morendo	*Mo-ren'doh*	Dying

LETTERS, TERMS AND SIGNS OF EMPHASIS (*Continued*)

TERM	PRONUNCIATION	MEANING
Sforzando, *sf* or ∧	*Sfort-sahn'doh*	Attacked with
Rinforzando, *rf* or >	*Reen-fort-sahn'doh*	sudden force
Sforzato assai, *sff* or *sfz* >	*Sfort-sah'toh as-sah'ee*	With exceeding strength
Marcato	*Marr-kah'toh*	Markedly
Ben marcato	*Ben marr-kah'toh*	Well marked
Pesante, or —	*Pay-sahn'tay*	Heavily, impressively
Martellato	*Marr-tel-lah'toh*	Hammered, suddenly, forcibly

Crescendo   Diminuendo

As application of the foregoing is relative, not absolute, much is left to the taste of the player, or conductor, each of whom is required to decide the tone force best suited to this or that section, phrase or period. Exercise of discrimination in this respect marks the work of the careful musician, in what may be termed the conventional technique of musical dynamics. Study of the foregoing in all varying gradations is worthy of serious attention, more especially as they are only relative.

Intimately associated with the study of dynamics in their various relations is the subject of "pitch." More or less difficulty is experienced in maintaining even pitch, when passing through the various modifications or gradations of tone force, or in sustained efforts of *piano* and *forte*. Sudden accessions or diminutions will be marked by heightening or lowering of pitch, unless ears and intelligence be on the alert to counteract the tendency. Particularly is care needed where sudden transitions from loud to soft or soft to loud occur, at a point in the composition where the melody, or part, proceeds by an interval of some magnitude, and the dynamic contrast is thus emphasized by sudden elevation or descent in tonal compass. There is always danger that the *forte* will be too flat, especially if it be sudden and not cumulative, as the result of a *crescendo*, the reason for which is that sudden, increased pressure of wind through the lips affects the tension necessary to maintain correct intonation.

Again, increase and decrease of tonal force, gradual or sudden, are marked in the performance of many instrumentalists by irregular fingering and retardation or acceleration of time, the general tendency being to hurry or slacken speed with accession or falling off in strength; while the *forte* invites hastening, the *piano* inclines to lingering. These faults are pointed out as likely to occur in compositions where the time should, generally speaking, be strict. Music of an emotional character, wherein the *tempo rubato* prevails, demands dynamic treatment peculiar to itself, for there license apparently reigns supreme and the law of uniformity is ignored. This style is exceptional, and may become very effective in the hands of a skillful artist, or director who has all shades of dynamic expression under complete control.

There is much in connection with the contemplation of dynamic guides that does not appear at first sight, but which careful study will develop. Their indications should be regarded as of primary importance, for the play of their varying qualities is unquestionably of im-

portance in enhancing the effect of a composition, just
as much so as diversity of light and shade on the central
figure of a painting.

The unwritten law of dynamics takes account of in-
flections, modifications, emphases not indicated by conventional words or signs, but felt to be necessary to
perfect development of a composition and its artistic,
if not always ideal, interpretation. The equation of personal taste enters here, but other than it the consideration deals with the expressive element, the inner spirit
of a work and the intent of the composer.

There are not, nor can be, any indications for those
dynamic subtleties of expression which heighten the
emotional character of a composition, because the intensity and force of *nuance* varies in each phrase and period
as does the play of sunlight on rippling water. No two
performers render the same passage in like manner with
respect to tonal force and accent. Each one delivers it
with the passion or power he personally feels to be suitable to its inner meaning, and were it possible to grade
intensity and underlying intent by mathematical signs
and figures, it would still remain the same. In music the
emotional nature of man must have full play; it cannot
be trammeled by pedantic rules, but may be directed by
education. A refined, educated musician will express
himself in music with elegance of diction as does the
cultured orator. The grammar of art may have influenced his style, directed his energies and assisted the
development of his talent, but has not suppressed his

individuality. Operative in all he renders, there is no more trace of stiffness or pedantry than is to be found in the lovely, chaste figures of a sculptor, wherein rigidity of mathematical proportions, softened by art, becomes graceful and pleasing to the eyes. Efforts of the uncultivated musician abound in crudities; those of the unimaginative, painstaking musician are pervaded by the spirit of neatness, regularity, precision, everything as specified and always strictly according to rule, no more nor less; but those of the musician of imagination, of soul, are full of spiritual meaning, and rule and order become the handmaids of art to assist its outer manifestation. He becomes the medium to interpret the composer's thoughts, the deliverer of a message to mankind, and thus by influence of the higher power with whom his own nature is in harmony, sways the emotions of mankind, entreating, coaxing, arousing, exciting, dominating each in turn, as it comes to him in the mood of the message he interprets.

Artistic renderings of musical dynamics, in their endless gradations, visibly indicated or invisibly suggested, apparent in skillful performance, are difficult to describe. The visible are concrete blocks, but the invisible are as impalpable as ether; they pulse around us; we are cognizant of their existence, realize their influence, but cannot grasp their substance. A noted writer approximately describes the elements of artistic dynamics in the following words, wherein cause is stated but effect left unexplained: "Every composition and every phrase requires the sonority of intensity of sound suitable to its structure. The *nuances*, therefore, embrace not only the rhythms, note for note, but the whole of a musical composition from its first to its last phrase. They form the cement or link which unites, connects, and combines these different dynamic elements." To test this, take some unfamiliar melody and copy it without time signature, bar lines and dynamic indications; play it through according to your own ideas, as to occurrence of time, nuance, increase and decrease of intensity, etc., then compare your rendering with the original indications. This experiment will assist in the realization that music is dependent for its expression not only on visible indications, but also on that impalpable something which, for want of a better term, is termed " taste " or " style."

Efforts to heighten musical declamation, laudable as they are, unless kept within bounds are liable to exaggeration and abuse. To rise to their full level of usefulness they must appear as the spontaneous ebullition of a deeply artistic nature upon which education has exercised its corrective influence. There must be no striving after effect for effect's sake, but everything must appear natural, and just what this note, section, phrase or period seems to demand for its proper dynamic utterance. Persons will differ in their reading of music as others do in prose or poetry. Those variations enphasize the fact that each earnest man imbues the work in hand with his own personality. In the world of players it cannot be pointed out where any two men agree precisely as to *tempo* or intensity, even in some well-known composition, and that is why we hear of the reading of this or that work by a certain conductor differing from that of another. These differences are often minute, in fact may be so trifling as to pass unobserved by an average person, but undeniably present and appreciable by the cultured musician, to whom they convey a world of meaning. A gentle emphasis on some note, or a heavy accentuation on another, will change the character of an entire phrase, just as an inflexion on some word in prose will alter, and mayhap subvert, the meaning of a sentence.

In bygone times some composers gave neither indications of *tempo* nor dynamic force, leaving the discovery of both to the performer. Modern editions of those works, edited by musicians of recognized standing, supply the deficiencies. These editions illustrate difference of opinion, and thus show that the deepest study of certain musical problems will not lead to precisely identical results. Yet any one or all of them may be accepted as guides, nothing more, to a reading which may be considered conformable with artistic traditions, if not exactly in unison with the composer's own ideas.

The subject of musical dynamics is a broad one, well worthy a volume rather than a chapter, for in reality it reaches from the foundation to the superstructure and to the roof tree, including within its scope every gradation of expression to be derived from the application of varying degrees of force as applied to the single note or germ; a completed composition, or any and all of its component

parts. The man who, claiming that he has attained perfection by faithful application of all the words and
signs indicating musical dynamics, misses more than half
the requirement, and stops short of midway to the goal
which he professes to have reached. The remaining
points to be gained are not set down on any chart; they
are spiritual, hence invisible. That, perhaps, is why he
does not appreciate them.

The following table, in outline somewhat resembling an
East Indian pagoda, is based on the carrying power of
the tone of each instrument named. As a general rule,
the more rapid the vibration of musical sounds the more
quickly they dissipate themselves by friction. Compare
the incisive tone of the piccolo or the sound of a pistol
with the profound tone of a BB♭ bass or reverberations
of a cannon. Comparison of the number of dotted lines
in any one section with those in another will give some
idea of the relative strength of tone subsisting between
them, and thus may be gained a fair conception —
instrument for instrument — of tone-balancing in the
wind-band.

Naturally, such a chart can convey an approximate
idea, only, of dynamic relativity of the several instruments named. Nevertheless, the attempt to measure
the mental effect and make it apparent to the eye,
will, it is hoped, conduce to a better understanding of
instrumental tonal proportions than at present obtains
among students and the music-loving but unskilled
public.

TABLE SUGGESTING RELATIVE POWER VALUE AMONG
VOICES OF INSTRUMENTS IN THE WIND-BAND.

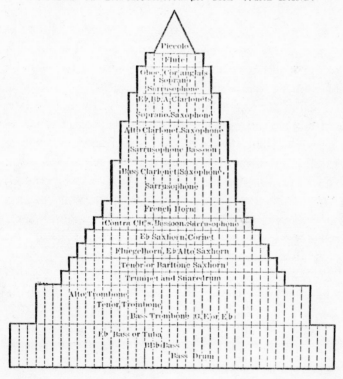

CHAPTER XV

TECHNIQUE

LIMITED application of the term *technique* (Fr.) is synonymous with digital facility. Its broader significance implies all elements entering into, or being combined in, musical performance on the plane of mechanical exposition, or expression.

Digital facility is acquired by study and practice of methods of fingering, usual and exceptional, pertaining to all notes within the compass of an instrument. By this is intended that fingering commonly taught as applying to each note of the scale shall be supplemented by knowledge of exceptional methods, as shown to be possible from acquaintance with the harmonic nature of individual instruments. For instance, there are four ways to finger E, third space, treble clef, on the cornet and other brass instruments, thus: o, first and second, or third, or first, second and third valves. (The latter is much out of tune.) Wood-wind instruments, also, present many exceptional fingerings. Upper fifths and octaves, etc., on flute, oboe, saxophone, may be forced from the finger positions of a lower octave, as shown by the law of harmonics. The low B♭ and its twelfth above (F), middle B and C, G♯, B♭, C, C♯ and D above the staff, all serve to illustrate what the clarionet has to offer in the way of exceptional fingerings. How, when, or where to adopt this or that fingering of a note, or series of notes, should be thought out diligently and systematically, for command of that knowledge will often help to remove difficulties involved in fingering certain passages in the ordinary manner.

Fingers must move freely, but never should the hand, as a whole, be permitted to partake of their movement. To see a player whose hand shares in the vertical action of the fingers, whose wrists and elbows are raised from an easy and natural position in endeavoring to execute a trill, is to witness a most ungraceful sight. Besides being ungraceful and awkward these movements impede execution and make it irregular in flow. Mechanical contrivances, similar in purpose with the "technicon" for the piano, supplemented by a well-devised series of finger gymnastics, would greatly aid in the acquirement of digital facility and correctness of method and position.

Blowing comes under the head of technique. Connection between blowing and production of sound is apparent, but every player does not appear to realize that this action may be brought entirely under control for expression of amplitude and quality through all gradations of dynamic intensity and in every shade of tone color. Energy in blowing may be so conserved by judicious practice as to reduce the labor involved, in sound production, to a minimum. The loudest sound in our immediate neighborhood is often not the one which carries farthest, neither is it the most musical. Sound homogeneous in all its elements, consequently musical, besides being delightful to the ears, will be heard at greater distance than a complex sound, or noise of equal dynamic intensity. Steady wind pressure, no matter which the dynamic sign, is an indispensable condition. Variation of force is one of degree only, and the requirement of an even, steady pressure of breath into the tube knows no modification. Rigidness of the foregoing requirement is not mitigated by *crescendo*, *diminuendo*, or any form of emphasis, for unless pressure of air from the lungs be steady, no such thing as perfect augmentation and diminution of sustained tones, or *legato* passages, can be obtained. In *staccato* the flow of breath is checked by the movement of the tongue at intervals of more or less rapid occurrence, but this check is in the nature of a pulsation only, which should not be permitted to affect steadiness of force, otherwise the tone quantity will become spasmodic and lacking in unity. Cultivation of the *cantabile* style of playing acts as deterrent to the formation of a jerky style of playing and enhances the charm of instrumental performance by its approach to good vocalism.

Firmness of embouchure is most essential; without it, true pitch cannot be steadily maintained. The term "embouchure" is employed to designate: (1) the part of a wind instrument applied to the mouth; (2) disposition of lips, tongue and other contiguous organs and muscles operating together in the effort to produce a musical sound. "To the embouchure is due," writes

W. H. Stone, "not only the correct quality of sound produced, but also slight variations in pitch which enable the player to preserve accurate intonation." Correction of the "slight variations" referred to is known among musicians variously as "humoring," or "nursing."

When the mouthpiece of a brass instrument is applied to the mouth, the lips form a pair of elastic cushions between its face and the teeth. Technically the lips vibrate when playing, with rapidity necessary to the pitch of any given note; but this change of rapidity is coincident with more or less alteration of the lips and readjustment of the facial muscles. Control of embouchure enables the player to (1) draw the lips tightly across the teeth, or to slacken them; (2) to compress or extend the orifice between the lips at will; and (3) to prevent escape of wind from the angles of the mouth. This unconscious process of stretching, slackening, compressing or extending goes on continually while the musician is playing, and no two sounds, be they only a semitone apart, can be produced without involving one or more of those movements. Position of embouchure varies from that of a firm normal condition for medium tones, to one considerably relaxed for low sounds, or of greatly compressed tension for high ones. For each sound there is only one position suitable to its accurate intonation. If the adjustment be not precise, pitch will be too flat or too sharp, as the lips are too much relaxed or tightened for its expression. The embouchure should be at once firm, elastic and sensitive. Care must be taken to guard against depreciation of pitch incident to "attack" of any note, for the tendency of the wind, on its passage, is to force the embouchure out of position, and if the lips be not properly adjusted at the moment of attack and prepared for resistance, the wind force will relax them and thus affect the intonation. From similar cause, there is always some difficulty in preserving accurate pitch during progress of the *crescendo* or *diminuendo*. It is necessary that intelligence shall coöperate with the embouchure in direction of each other mechanical operation involved in performance. Cultivation of the faculty for thinking sounds will be found valuable, for thereby form, substance and position become as mental pictures, to be transferred with accuracy and made manifest by the accomplishment of technique.

Cultivation of the perception of pitch, in its most minute differentiations, is a very essential element of wind-instrument technique. Average aural capacity is by no means sufficient for the musician, whose hearing should be supersensitive to a degree. He is operating under enactments of the most exacting character and giving musical expression to the laws of mathematics as applied to sound. The practice in general of leaving it all — or most of it — to the instrument is altogether wrong, for wind instruments — even the best — are inherently defective, and for that reason alone make great demand upon the aural capacity of, and embouchure control by, the player.

Study of scales, chords and intervals, undertaken

intelligently for development of tone, sense of hearing, digital facility and other qualities, is essential to perfect technique, without which there can be no such thing as pure harmony, true dynamic expression, smooth fingering or exact time in the wind-band.

CHAPTER XVI

ENSEMBLE

The term *ensemble*, borrowed from the French, signifies, "(1) the general effect of a musical performance; (2) the union of the whole company of performers in a concerted piece."

Some of the most important elements contributory to perfect ensemble are rhythmic impulse, appropriate *tempo*, smooth execution, correct intonation, dynamic mobility, good tone color and refined expression.

By rhythmic impulse is meant the impetus given to performance by correct accentuation; (1) according to the division of the measure; (2) in keeping with the phrasal construction of the melody, especially where, as is frequently the case, this quality dominates and takes precedence over the regular up and down dual or triple accent indicated by the time signature; and (3) the occasional or irregular accent interposed with design of introducing a rhythmic impulse at variance with expected grouping of the measure. In all instances wherein several players are taking part together, the attack and delivery of each quality of accent must be coincident; also the fractional divisions of notes into which rhythm and measure are divided must appear on the same instant of time and with correctness of melodic flow. Cultivation

of keen perception for duration value of notes in their
varying proportions is a desideratum which must not
be neglected. Hesitating attack of metric or rhythmic
accent, anticipation or delay of entry, misplaced accent,
as is common where rhythms begin with initial or starting
notes, and again where groups of notes in their rise and
fall suggest an accentuation differing from that required
by the time signature, are all faulty, as:

which, suggesting a dual rhythm, would be rendered by a
careless player as though written for the most part in ⅝
time, thus:

Again, where division is by groups of three notes, there
often appears diversity in delivery, injuriously affecting
ensemble, as, ¾ ♪♪♪ ♪♪♪ , which is not infrequently
rendered ¾ ♪♪♪ ♪♪♪. The foregoing examples will
suggest many other confusing enunciations brought
about by thoughtless players, who, though they may be

in the minority, will cause a loss of clearness and thus create a condition of accentuation much to be deplored. In some orchestras, whose directors are careful and exacting, it is the custom to have the violins bow their phrases alike, each player moving his bow in the same direction at the moment required. This brings about uniformity of strength and precision of attack in phrasing. To insure this identity of movement the several points where doubt might exist are marked ∨ or ⊓, signifying up or down bow; and though this careful method is often sneered at as an over-refinement, there can exist no doubt among good musicians as to its desirability and beneficial effect. A similar practice should be adopted in the wind-band, by which identity of breathing points would be established, for want of conformity with that requirement results in bad phrasing, weakens attack, confuses delivery and thus, by irregularity of rhythmic impulse, injures the ensemble.

Tempo exercises an undoubted influence on rhythmic expression. Irrational modification of tempo, misconception as to speed appropriate to the composition as a whole, dragging, or hurrying in phrases or passages, each and all produce bad effects on ensemble. Schumann aptly described this irresolution of tempo as "resembling the gait of a drunken man." The value of playing in time, and the habit of faithfully following the indications of the conductor, cannot be overestimated, nor too strongly impressed on the attention of members of the wind-band.

Regularity of execution is connected with the requirements of tempo, for to large extent they are interdependent. Confusion of rhythmic divisions, uneven flights of notes of greater or less extent, conduce to unsteadiness of tempo. The law designed to regulate the position of the fractional elements of a measure, in relation one with the other, should be regarded as inexorable in the operation of its primary but essential requirement. Modifications are bound to appear; at no time ought they to result from caprice, but, on the contrary, such exceptions to the law must justify their nonconformity, by evidence of the presence of a higher mandate of sound, artistic taste or judgment. Under any circumstance, smoothness of *technique*, with all that word implies, remains a constant essential of perfect ensemble in collective playing by the wind-band.

Exact agreement in pitch, or tune, between the several instruments of an organization is necessary. The science of music teaches that complex vibrations produce noise, and that simple, regular or periodic vibrations result in music. Defective intonation among instruments sets up a condition of complex vibrations, and the greater the departure from tonal exactness, the nearer its approach to noise. Musical laws are extremely strict in their application to pitch, allowing for no deviation from an exact standard. If 256 vibrations be required to produce a note at a certain pitch on one instrument, the same number will be necessary with another; $255\frac{3}{4}$ or $256\frac{1}{8}$ vibrations will not do; the requirement of strict con-

formity is absolute in each and every note of the scale.
There is nothing haphazard in the matter of musical
pitch; its requirements are based on the mathematical
and proportional vibratory relation of all sounds in the
full scale with the fundamental tone of our musical
system. "Beats" among the lower instruments of slow
vibrations, equally with trill-like quivering inaccuracy
among the higher ones with rapid vibrations, should not
be permitted; they are certainly ruinous to ensemble.

Intensity of sound has its bearing upon tone color, for
tones overforced or too feebly incited lose in character of
quality. Subtleties of shades of intensity in infinite variety, like tints of color at the disposal of the painter, are
available to the musician and should be under his control.
In concerted playing, discretion must govern the efforts
of each instrumentalist, otherwise the tones of the larger
instruments will dominate those of the smaller ones
and destroy their effect. One coarse, loud tone from a
single instrument in a movement designed to be rendered
smoothly and softly will ruin the ensemble; one flaw has
depreciated the value of the diamond.

Musicians, by the hundred, speak of expression as
though the total of its requirements were summed up in
attention to words and signs used to signify gradations
of dynamic intensity. Expression, in the broader sense,
implies enunciation of a composition in whole, or in its
component parts, in accordance with the writer's intent
and inner meaning. Abnegation of personal idiosyncrasy
to demands of composer and conductor is the spirit in

which the wind-band player should approach his work. Many players seem loath to merge their individuality into that of the conductor, yet experience teaches that a strict, one-man dictatorship, tolerating no approach to musical insubordination, is essential to a homogeneous performance by any body of players. The more they realize this fact, the better will be the ensemble playing of the organization with which they are identified.

CHAPTER XVII

ANTOINE JOSEPH SAX

MENTION of the name Sax has been so frequent in the course of this book as, no doubt, to awaken curiosity as to the career and achievements of that talented man, who, above all, deserves to be revered and remembered as Father of modern wind instrument structure. To, in some measure, satisfy that legitimate curiosity the following sketch, written immediately subsequent to his death, Feb. 9, 1894, is presented:

Antoine Joseph Sax was born at Dinant, Belgium, Nov. 6, 1814, his father being the celebrated instrument maker, Charles Joseph Sax, whose labors to improve the clarionet and inventions connected with brass instruments had won for him a prominent position among the *luthiers* of Belgium. Antoine, sometimes referred to as Adolphe, early displayed a taste for the vocation of his father, and also manifested great musical ability. The father took special care to foster those inclinations, affording the lad every encouragement in the workshop, as well as directing his studies in music. When old enough he entered the Brussels Conservatoire de Musique and studied the clarionet and flute. Under the celebrated master, Bender, he acquired great skill on the clarionet, but seems never to have applied it in a professional capacity. His predilections took him back to the workshop, where he labored diligently along the lines laid down by his father for perfecting the clarionet family, greatly improving the bass clarionet and inventing the double bass as a foundation for the same. Throughout the whole of his subsequent career he devoted much attention to these instruments, and was so successful in his endeavors as to attract the attention and commendation of Hector Berlioz, who thus refers to him in his "Treatise on Modern Instrumentation and Orchestration" (London edition, 1858): "The manufacture of these instruments, which remained for so long in its infancy, is nowadays in a state of progress which cannot fail to bring the most valuable results; already great advance has been made by M. Adolphe Sax, the skillful and accomplished Parisian manufacturer." He then proceeds to describe some of the improvements effected by Sax, some of which, such as adding a semitone to the lower compass of the clarionet, causing it to descend to E♭, are now no longer generally known. The remarks made by Berlioz were written a few years after Sax had left Dinant and settled permanently at Paris, which he did in 1842. He opened a modest workshop in the Rue St. George, but so great was his superiority over all instrument makers then resident in that city, that he found it speedily necessary greatly to enlarge his premises, owing to the numerous orders intrusted to him by professional musicians and others.

At the time Sax appeared in Paris, brass instruments were in a deplorable state. How imperfect their condition may be judged by the following quotation from a "Method for Saxhorn and Saxotromba," the writer of which remarks: "No coherence, no unity between the individual members of the group, in one case keys, in another valves, a small compass, an imperfect scale, lack of accurate intonation throughout, bad quality of tone, variations of fingering requiring fresh study in passing from one instrument to another. The keyed bugle, built on false proportions, offered no prospect of improvement; the mechanism of the valves themselves, by their abrupt angles, deteriorated the quality of tone, and the absence of intermediate instruments caused gaps in the general scale, and at times false combinations."

These evils Sax perceived, and directed every effort of his genius to overcome. Two years after taking up his residence at Paris (1844), he won a silver medal for his display of brass and wood instruments at the French Exhibition. One year later he took out patents for his saxhorn, an improved form of bugle, and "for a family of cylinder instruments called saxotrombas, intermediate between the saxhorn and the cylinder trumpet." Each of these instruments was characterized by material change in prevailing models and immense improvements in acoustical construction. Further, he organized brass instruments into groups, obtaining a corresponding tonal quality from lowest to highest in each group, and greatly improved the mechanism of the piston. His saxhorn family, the prototype of our modern brass-band instruments, consisted of at least seven members: soprano in

F, E♭ and D, contraltos in C and B♭, tenors in F and E♭, baritones in C and B♭, basses in F and E♭ and contrabasses, circular in form, in BB♭. As well in form as in name these instruments have undergone change since their invention by Sax, but in essential principles they remain the same to-day as then, and, it must be added, no improvement of later times has taken place that was not suggested if not positively initiated by this great maker. For instance, duplicate (duplex) "bells" for brass instruments, increase in number of valves, and, above all, the system of valve "compensators" by which it is sought to improve their intonation, of which we see and hear so much in these days, were invented or introduced over a half century ago by Sax.

In 1846 he patented the invention with which his name still continues to be connected, viz., the saxophone. This instrument, with a mouthpiece similar to that of a clarionet, has a conical brass tube, pierced with holes at acoustical intervals, which for convenience in playing are covered by keys and finger plates. It is an instrument of hybrid tonal quality, having in that respect affinity with the single reed, as well as the cupped-mouthpiece groups. The peculiar character of its tone fits it more as a component of the wind-band than of the orchestra. He made a complete quartet of saxophones, viz., B♭ soprano, E♭ alto, B♭ tenor and E♭ bass, and thus gave four new voices to the world of music.

Jealous of his achievements, there have not been wanting men of less caliber to dispute his claims as improver, originator, inventor, notable among whom may be mentioned Wieprecht and Cerveny, but without success, decisions in court being invariably in favor of Sax.

He was fortunate to find friends at Court, and as a result secured a practical monopoly for the supply of wind instruments of his manufacture to the French army. At the Paris Industrial Exhibition of 1894 he was awarded a gold medal, and at the great Exhibition of 1851 he obtained the Conseil d'Exposition medal for the three families of instruments with which his name was identified.

In 1852 he became bankrupt, but by arrangement with his creditors recommenced business. In 1859, owing to the reformation of pitch, every military band and orchestra in France had to procure new wind instruments. "An enormous advantage," remarks a writer in Grove's "Dictionary of Music and Musicians," "by which any one else in Sax's place would have made a fortune; but with all his ability and shrewdness he was not a man of business, and his affairs became hopelessly involved. From that time his affairs went from bad to worse, and though he exhibited at London in 1862, and took the Grand Prize at Paris in 1867, his tide of fortune continued to ebb. His factory at Paris passed out of his hands, his collection of musical instruments was dispersed, and in fact nearly all by which he set store was scattered by the inexorable hand of fate and the auctioneer's hammer."

The life of Sax furnishes an illustration of the fact that possession of genius does not always lead to fortune, and even though by combination of circumstances and assistance of powerful friends, as in this case, the man of genius may succeed in obtaining a foothold on the coveted wheel, he usually completes the revolution instead of stepping off on the high level when half the round is made. There was a time in the history of Sax when he might have retired with a snug competence, if not great fortune. Friends in high quarters, assistance of prominent musicians, such as Berlioz, Halévy and Kastner, favorable comments of the French press and, in fact, the applause of all Europe, placed him in a position to which few men attain in middle life. Having reached that point his wheel of fortune began the downward half of its revolution; competition, litigation, above referred to, and poor business capacity, so loaded it that the descent was rapid, and the wheel was too heavily weighted ever to rise again. Thus it came about that the man to whom wind instrumentalists and modern *facteurs* are so deeply indebted for improvements and inventions died at Paris, in the eightieth year of his age, almost penniless and well-nigh forgotten.

ACKNOWLEDGMENTS

List of works referred to in the preparation of this book to which the author acknowledges indebtedness:

History of Music	W. A. Chappell, F.S.A.
The Philosophy of Music	Wm. Pole, F.R.S. Mus. Doc., Oxon.
The Scientific Basis of Music	W. Stone
Handbook of Acoustics	J. Broadhouse
Instrumentation and Orchestration	H. Berlioz
Manuel Général de Musique Militaire	G. Kastner
Military Music	J. A. Kappey
Le Polycorde	J. F. Giraud
Musical Instruments	C. Engle
Various magazine articles on wind instruments, notably nearly the whole of Chapter IV	F. A. Mahan, Major U. S. A. (Retired)
Dictionary of Music and Musicians	Sir George Grove
Musical Expression	M. Lussy

If there are others, inadvertently omitted — apologies!

INDEX